"Having worked with Values-based Education for many years, as a long-term associate of VbE, I find *The Conscious Classroom* to be a definitive guide for the modern educator. Having introduced and embedded VbE, both in the trenches as a Headteacher and later as a Multi-Academy Trust leader, I have seen the transformative power of VbE in action.

"In our Trust, Values-based Education has been the place where we have found alignment with all our schools and the place where we continue to grow our collaboration. With first-hand experience of developing and deepening VbE in our classrooms, we have built a cohesive ethos across our group of schools where students develop the ethical intelligence and agency to navigate an AI-driven world. This book is not just theory; it is a roadmap to creating the harmony, resilience and wellbeing that our children – and our society – so desperately need."

Cori Bateman, *Chief Executive Officer, Pioneer Learning Trust*

"I have known Neil for many years, and I can say this without hesitation. This book is the purest expression of who he is as a human being and as an educator. I have travelled the world with Neil, shared stages with him, sat in deep conversations late into the night, and watched him quietly transform rooms full of teachers and leaders, simply by the way he listens and speaks from the heart.

"*The Conscious Classroom* is not a theory-heavy manifesto. It is a grounded, deeply human invitation to rethink what education is really for. Neil reminds us that schools are not just places to pass exams, but places where character, wisdom and ethical leadership are formed. His thinking feels urgently relevant in a world that often feels loud, polarised and disconnected.

"This book will challenge you, reassure you and inspire you in equal measure. If you care about children, wellbeing and the future of humanity, this is essential reading."

Gavin McCormack, *Award winning teacher, co-founder of Upschool*

"*The Conscious Classroom* is a visionary approach to education and leadership. Neil's insights offer a compassionate and practical pathway to nurturing ethical intelligence, equipping both educators and students with the tools needed to thrive in today's complex world. This book is an inspiring guide for anyone seeking to create lasting positive change in schools and beyond."

Dr Mark Williams, *Neuroscience Professor, Keynote Speaker, Author*

"Here is an inspiring book which will help every leader to think, talk with others and act to develop their school . . . consciously. It provides a fund of good advice, examples of effective practice and an invitation to put children first in all we do."

Professor Mick Waters, *Curriculum Expert*

"Dr Neil Hawkes' latest book, *The Conscious Classroom*, is an essential read for any teacher, educational leader or lawmaker. Neil Hawkes brings a lifetime of experience, built around teaching, leadership and research, to the wisdom found in the concept of ethical intelligence. Ethical intelligence is about a superior consciousness grounded in self-knowing and empathy, the veritable stuff of personal, social and moral wellbeing, according to the most recent neuroscientific insights. The concept presents as a challenge to the many systems of education worldwide currently disposed to instrumentalist aims and objectives, ones focussed on easily measurable goals of a basic consciousness that is fast becoming the domain of artificial intelligence. Ethical intelligence is about a truly human consciousness well beyond the bounds of AI. The book offers both the theory and multiple practical examples of how this can be achieved in the classroom, along with its many personal and social benefits."

Emeritus Professor Terence Lovat, *The University of Newcastle, Australia, The University of Oxford, UK, The University of Johannesburg, South Africa*

The Conscious Classroom

The Conscious Classroom draws on both the author's deep and comprehensive experience of schools and the incredible work of educators who are helping students to develop greater critical and creative awareness in classrooms. This solutions-focused book offers a pathway to mental wellbeing and ethical leadership and will enable schools to nurture those aspects of character that enable students to have an awakened conscience, rooted in a clear understanding and living of values, such as dignity, compassion, integrity, justice, trust and harmony.

This work is actively informed by neuroscience and what is now known about how our brains best learn and describes how students can be more consciously aware in a process of developing the essential skill of self-leadership, which nourishes resilience, wellbeing and agency. Its central question for adults and students alike is, "Who do you choose to be in the world?" Neil gives a fascinating overview, explaining how his original ideas emerged as a teacher, headteacher and leader of school systems. He explains how values, reflective thinking and quality education are the keys to expanding consciousness, wellbeing and self-leadership. The book focuses on ten schools that demonstrate how they are creating *conscious classrooms*.

This essential book will help teachers to enhance the wellbeing and resilience of themselves and their students and give hope and a sense of renewed purpose to those who believe in the power of education for the general good of humanity.

Neil Hawkes is a globally recognised educator, speaker, broadcaster, author and social commentator. He is a former Head Teacher and County Education Adviser in the UK and has influenced educational policy and practice worldwide. He is a popular TEDx presenter and a member of the V20 Task Group advising G20 leaders on values.

Neil Hawkes

The Conscious Classroom

A Pathway to Mental Wellbeing and Ethical Leadership

Routledge
Taylor & Francis Group
LONDON AND NEW YORK

Designed cover image: © Getty Images

First published 2027
by Routledge
4 Park Square, Milton Park, Abingdon, Oxon OX14 4RN

and by Routledge
605 Third Avenue, New York, NY 10158

Routledge is an imprint of the Taylor & Francis Group, an informa business

British Library Cataloguing-in-Publication Data
A catalogue record for this book is available from the British Library

ISBN: 978-1-041-15780-9 (hbk)
ISBN: 978-1-041-15768-7 (pbk)
ISBN: 978-1-003-68114-4 (ebk)

DOI: 10.4324/9781003681144

Typeset in Bembo
by Apex CoVantage, LLC

The Conscious Classroom *contains my lifetime's mission for a better world and is dedicated to the children of the future, who will be holding up the world with their values, having been educated in Conscious Classrooms.*

Contents

Welcome from Neil

Welcome to *The Conscious Classroom – A Pathway to Mental Wellbeing and Ethical Leadership*. I have written this book from my heart, because I am passionate about promoting a form of quality education that empowers young people to realise their innate potential. It has evolved from my many years of visiting schools all over the world. I hope that it will be both an inspirational read and a resource for enhancing consciousness in whatever setting you find yourself.

You may be wondering why I choose to differentiate between classrooms and *conscious classrooms*. After all, aren't the people in all classrooms 'conscious'? Yes, they are, in the sense that human beings possess consciousness, meaning that they are aware that they are alive, with subjective experiences, thoughts and feelings. A conscious classroom deliberately fosters a heightened state of consciousness that enables students to be aware of their essence as human beings and to be alert as reflective, creative, critical learners, basing their thoughts and actions on human values such as dignity, respect, justice, truth, compassion and integrity.

You may ask, why are such classrooms needed? Surely classrooms are about imparting knowledge, practising skills and being inducted into subject disciplines, then testing students to determine whether they have learned their lessons and using their exam results to decide what work to take up.

This traditional model is past its sell-by date and needs a radical overhaul, as it doesn't prepare students to understand themselves and the world in which they now live. Yes, of course, they need to have a range of basic skills, to be literate, numerate and inspired to understand our world through literature, the arts, sciences and humanities. But with the advent of AI, we have created an intelligence that students can use to find information and help them perform so many tasks.

If what I'm suggesting is correct, then we need to change the balance in classrooms to ensure that students are developing a full range of human intelligences. Intelligences that give them the ability to be in control of their thinking and behaviour in a way that is of benefit to them and also for the greater good of society.

Observing world events, it can be felt that a few high-profile leaders and their media outlets control the fate of the rest of us. They often focus on division and polarisation, fuelling hate and failing to recognise that all people share the same humanity and deserve to be treated with dignity and respect. Their behaviour creates civil unrest and war. Ordinary people, like you and me, may be fooled by their promises to solve our problems if we vote for them and join with them against others, whom they label as the enemy. Social media, and its algorithms, reinforces their prejudices by feeding us information that supports their views, such as boys being targeted with information that supports misogyny – a hatred of girls.

What humanity desperately needs is a new form of leadership, which is ethically intelligent, based on wisdom.

To herald this new form of leadership and governance, I'm proposing that we educate our young people to acquire the dispositions of character that will nurture their *ethical intelligence* – their ability to ethically self-regulate their thinking and behaviour. This form of education enhances the natural essence of us, which is based on human values such as empathy, compassion, love, peace and care. As the cognitive neuroscientist Mark Williams in Australia points out, we have survived as a species because we make good connections – we are at heart co-operative, caring social beings. Yes, we also have a shadow side as part of our human nature, but I believe that in acknowledging it and coming alongside it, we can transform those aspects of us that feed on limiting values such as greed, mistrust, envy, jealousy and intolerance.

Over the last few decades, I have been promoting a form of education which can give students access to a new consciousness, which provides the foundation for their mental wellbeing and leadership at all levels in society. My mission has been based on my research at Oxford University whilst working as the headteacher of a state community school that was the focus of my research.

This unique book will take you on a journey, which will give you an understanding of the principles behind the creation of conscious classrooms. My aim is to inspire you, so that you will understand the truth in my arguments and become an active part of my 'quiet revolution' of education.

After introducing you to the theory and practices of a conscious classroom, I will share with you my ten incredible insights, which are drawn from observing schools that I call *conscious schools*. These schools are creating opportunities for students to develop their ethical intelligence and consequently be capable of being *ethical leaders*, no matter what job or role they have in society.

These pioneering schools focus on enhancing *human values*, such as integrity, trust, compassion, justice and dignity, as the foundation of character development. They draw on an active understanding of a full range of human intelligences (which AI currently can't do), such as emotional, critical, creative, aesthetic, spiritual and physical intelligence, which I maintain lead to the formation of personal wisdom. I see wisdom as the ability for students to use their knowledge, experience, understanding, emotions and insights to make sound judgements. These judgements lead to making decisions, especially about complex life matters, that have an altruistic focus on the long-term wellbeing of themselves and others.

It is my hope that conscious classrooms will become the standard for all classrooms. As you will discover, my vision is already a reality in so many schools that we are now nearing a tipping point! With your support, we can transform the whole of the current educational system to be one that enables every student to flourish, because it nourishes their mental wellbeing and is ethically led.

Acknowledgements

The Conscious Classroom has been inspired by so many wonderful people, who have freely given their knowledge and wisdom about what a quality education should be so that our young people are educated to navigate successfully the complexities of their lives and those of society.

A huge thank you to all the leaders and schools that are mentioned in the text. You really are bringing the future into the present.

To the Values-based Education central team of Bridget Knight, Sue Jones, Nigel Cohen and Jane Hawkes, heartfelt thanks for all the generous, loving support you give me unconditionally, especially in strategically ensuring that schools, and other settings, embrace and benefit from the VbE philosophy and practices.

The IVET Foundation is the charity that holds the work of VbE so centrally to its mission and purpose, helping to create a values-led world. It has a remarkable team of patrons whose influence, scholarship and support are so valued by me and fellow trustees. Thank you: Sir John Jones; Professors Bart McGettrick, Mick Waters, Ruth Crick and Mark Chater; and Doctors Gladson Chickwa, Andrei Stupu and Tessa Willy. Also, to the memory of Professor Richard Pring, who died recently. Whilst my supervisor at Oxford University, Richard's influence on my thinking about ethics and life was profound.

ACKNOWLEDGEMENTS

To my fellow members of the founding team of the Global Alliance of Values-based Education (GAVE), a special thanks for creating a forum to which all values-based people and organisations can belong, so that we can work together for the flourishing of humanity. A huge thank you to Terry Lovat, Ron Toomey, Craig Shealy, and Ron and Suwanti Farmer.

A very special thank you to Lynn Henshall. Lynn is the secretary of Living Values Education in the British Isles, of which I am the chair. We have worked together in these roles for many years. Without Lynn's generosity of spirit and immeasurable proofreading skills, suggesting textual revisions and challenging what may be unclear to the reader, I would not have completed the manuscript to meet the publisher's deadline and high standards.

Thank you to the team at the Routledge | Taylor & Francis Group for commissioning me to write the book – very much appreciated.

Finally, I acknowledge the immense contribution that Jane Hawkes has made to the development of my understanding of the complexity of our inner worlds. Jane's expertise as a psychotherapist and her loving essence have had an immense influence on so many aspects of *The Conscious Classroom*.

About the author

Neil Hawkes at the UN in Geneva.
Neil Hawkes D. Phil (Oxford), MEd, BA, FRSA

Neil Hawkes is a doctoral graduate of Kellogg College, Oxford University. He is well known worldwide as an inspirational speaker, educator, broadcaster, author and social commentator. He is a popular TEDx presenter.

Neil's thinking is having a profound influence on education globally. Neil first gained international recognition when, after a successful career as a chief education adviser, he returned to being a headteacher in Oxfordshire, UK. Here he conducted research, with the support of Oxford University, to devise and implement a transformational model of education, which would give pupils an ethical vocabulary, based on universal human values such as respect, tolerance, humility and justice. The school community found that pupils were empowered to embody ethical intelligence, the ability to ethically self-regulate their thinking and behaviour. Pupils developed the capacity to be ethical leaders of themselves and others, displaying excellent behaviour and good character. The quality of their schoolwork was enhanced too because they took responsibility for their learning and had time for inner reflection. School staff modelled the school's values and reported that Values-based Education (VbE) had created an harmonious school community, which fostered wellbeing.

Today, VbE has spread into all aspects of society worldwide, and Neil is consulted by government agencies and school systems. He is one of the V20 Task Group of values experts who advise G20 leaders about the importance of values to humanity:

www.values20.org/wp-content/uploads/2022/02/2021-V20-Communique-and-Policy-Briefs-Sharing-Policy-Brief.pdf

He is one of the United Nations Institute for Training and Research (UNITAR) experts on ethical leadership and has spoken at the UN in Geneva.

To promote Values-based Living (VbL), Neil founded the International Values-based Trust (IVET Foundation) (*www.ivet-foundation.com*), with its educational arm Values-based Education (VbE) (*valuesbasededucation.com*). He is also one of the founders of the Global Alliance for Values-based Education (GAVE).

Neil's bestselling book, *From My Heart, Transforming Lives Through Values,* celebrates the success of VbE worldwide. With his wife Jane (a psychotherapist), he co-authored *The Inner Curriculum, How to Nurture Wellbeing, Resilience and Self-Leadership.* Neil feels that this latest book, *The Conscious Classroom – A Pathway to Mental Wellbeing and Ethical Leadership*, represents the tipping point of his influence to help transform schools.

Neil also hosts a podcast series, *Noble Conversations*, on major Internet platforms, where you can listen to inspiring conversations with people who are living their values and having an impact, often globally.

For more information, you can visit Neil's website at neilhawkes.org or search the Internet.

1

Your ideal classroom?

As you begin your journey with me through this book, a good starting point is for me to invite you to consider what your ideal classroom would be and what the crucial elements are that would make it ideal. Please see yourself as the architect of your future classroom, realising the power that you possess as a role model for your students.

I will provide prompts and pose questions that will enable you to construct a path that creates the conditions that will enrich the quality of learning in your classroom. The guiding principles of the conscious classroom will be signposts to the philosophy and practices of schools that describe themselves as having adopted *Values-based Education (VbE)* as their educational philosophy.

My aim is to inspire you, as one of the many heroes who are educating our children in an age of challenge, complexity and uncertainty.

DOI: 10.4324/9781003681144-1

Focus on YOU!

Because you are reading this book, I'm assuming that you are interested or involved with schools and education; perhaps, like me, you see the need for a transformation of the current limited system of educating children into one that will enable them to thrive personally and academically, by developing their character and ability to learn and giving them the capacity to build and live their unique qualities, values and behaviours, which will reflect their integrity and ethically based choices.

What gives me meaning and purpose for my life is to inspire educators to create classrooms and schools where students are educated in an ethos that will empower them to be more conscious; altruistically aware of themselves, others and the wider world. I argue that the result of such education is that students gain a special form of agency, being ethically self-led, navigating the challenges and complexity of their life. In other words, people who will ensure the flourishing of humanity and our beautiful world.

Also, you may be interested to read about some incredible schools that are creating conscious classrooms, and the benefits that they are bringing to their students and communities. You may be a teacher, teaching assistant, student teacher, school leader, administrator, academic, parent or community member. Whoever you are, you will probably have one thing in common: you will have experienced being a young person being educated in a classroom.

May I invite you to pause and take some time to think about: "What do you remember about your personal classroom experiences?"

Like me, I sense that you will have many thoughts and feelings about your experiences and the people who journeyed with you during your schooling. You may have a strong emotion triggered if you think of certain incidents or people, so please take care of you as you recall formational events. As you pause to remember, perhaps a teacher springs to your mind, like my Mr Smith, or the children who were in your school with you.

When I was seven, my teacher, Mr Smith, criticised a story that I had tried my best to write, and he remarked that I would never be a writer and that I was as stupid as my brother, who had previously been in his class. I cannot adequately tell you how much his cutting remark has lived with me over the years. I still carry some self-doubt and a feeling of uncertainty when I am writing – as I am experiencing even now.

My wife Jane is a psychotherapist. She tells me that I am not alone in having my sense of self influenced by a teacher when young. The most impressionable age is when we are under seven; generally, by this time, we have decided who we are in the world. Sadly, we carry this young version of ourselves into adult life, which can limit our self-perception and inner peace. Happily, we can be influenced by adults who build our self-confidence and help us to be the best versions of ourselves that we can be. Unfortunately, most of us can inadvertently make a remark or give a gesture, which acts like an arrow aimed at the heart of the child. I'm sure I may be guilty in the past of such unaware behaviour, so please don't put yourself on a guilt trip. Remember that we are building your classroom of the future, so please don't dwell on the past. In this present moment, we can only make a commitment to be more conscious of our words and actions. Making a commitment, to be more consciously aware, leads us on to thinking about who we are. I'm curious to know how you would reply if I asked you to explain who you are. Just pause for another few moments and think how you would reply if I asked, "Who are you?"

I wish I could hear your answer. However, let's briefly return the spotlight to me, "Who am I?"

If asked, I always describe myself by the role I'm most proud of being, and that is a teacher. This is because I'm honoured to be seen as one and to have the privilege of helping to create classrooms that enable children to flourish personally and academically. However, you could challenge my answer because I haven't said who I am, merely what I do, which is so often the response when asked this question.

At the 2025 Spirit of Humanity conference in Iceland, the President of Iceland, Halla Tómasdóttir, asked the audience a challenging question, which I believe is the more important question we should ask ourselves, "Who have I chosen to be in the world?"

Now, take time to consider how you would reply to this penetrating and revealing question . . .

Yes, for many of us it is a difficult question. Like me, I suspect you were sometimes asked the more familiar question, "What do you want to do when you grow up?" Therefore, we are not used to being asked to think deeply about who we are choosing to be, which makes us think about our character, personal qualities and values that drive our thinking and behaviour.

In simple terms, are you disposed to be kind and caring to others? Are you honest and trustworthy? Or do you behave in other ways, such as always putting yourself first? Do you criticise others or are often sarcastic? Or, like most of us, are you a mix of the two, depending on your mood and situation? Also, have you ever given yourself time to think about why you see others in the world in the way that you do? Where do your views, beliefs and attitudes, which make up your identity (your internal sense of yourself and your role in society) come from?

Who and how have people and experiences formed the person you present to the world?

A deep dive into such personal questions helps us to bring into awareness what generally remains unconscious. You may find it useful to share your thoughts with a trusted friend or member of the family, who may help you to gain clarity. If such thinking disturbs you, then it may be supportive to seek the advice of a counsellor or psychotherapist. I am lucky to be married to Jane, a skilled psychotherapist, who has helped me to understand and befriend my internal world.

As an inveterate people watcher, I have always been fascinated by such questions about who we are and why we do what we do in life. This intense curiosity became the impetus for creating a practical method of education that would empower young people to become fully conscious about why they think and behave in the way that they do. I wondered if there were tools and experiences that would help them to be the best version of themselves that they could be. For instance, they could gain clarity about any implicit biases they have about others which are outside their conscious awareness. Also, I was curious whether such thinking about increasing the personal awareness and consciousness of young people would improve the quality of education and improve the pro-social and academic outcomes of classrooms, schools, colleges and other settings.

The answer to my thoughts was a resounding YES! Drawing on the wisdom of many inspiring educators and leaders, my personal and professional journey gave me the transformational insights that formed my practical educational philosophy known as Values-based Education (VbE). Over the last thirty years, VbE has been adopted by countless schools worldwide. In many countries, values are now seen as an important ingredient of a successful curriculum; even by schools that have adopted values education, unaware of how and by whom it was introduced into the educational system.

In this book, you will discover how the basic tenets of VbE nourish learning environments that I now describe as conscious classrooms.

What is a conscious classroom?

I use the term *conscious classroom* to refer to the enhanced quality of self-understanding, relationships, curriculum, inclusion, classroom organisation, routines, structures and pedagogy that empowers students to be effective, happy, resilient life-long learners. Students are more aware, curious and reflective about themselves as human beings and their learning experiences as students. They are guided to make appropriate wise, ethical choices, underpinned by their understanding and practice of living life-enhancing values.

Students are encouraged to think of themselves as objective observers of what is happening, both internally in their minds and bodies and externally in their environment. Psychologists call this introspection; the process of observing and examining one's own conscious thoughts, which makes us more conscious, self-aware. To do this, students experience aspects of learning which strengthen their awareness, such as reflection, philosophy for children (P4C), art, drama, music, literature and physical education, enabling them to self-regulate their behaviour and be agents of their own learning. To support students in this process, teachers foster a learning environment based on dignity, the inherent self-worth of each student, by attending to their attachment needs, which are to feel safe, secure and, importantly, really seen. Students experience internal attunement; they feel integrated as people, cared for, recognised for who they are, giving them the sense of harmony with others and the world.

Neuroscience experts, such as Dr Dan Siegel, author of *The Mindful Brain* (WW Norton, 2007), explain what happens in our brains when this process occurs. For instance, integrative brain fibres wire up together in the brains of children who experience positive attachment with parents, teachers and themselves, giving them a sense of wellbeing. The conscious classroom replicates this process by uniquely teaching children how to strengthen their minds and have a positive attachment to themselves. They do this by monitoring their thoughts and feelings, so that they make connections with other people, and between aspects of experience and learning. This process enables them to enjoy a heightened level of awareness so that they can creatively work on the development of their character and be more diligent in their learning. A major outcome of a conscious classroom is student wellbeing, resilience and self-worth, because they experience internal harmony rather than chaos and rigidity, which sadly is the norm for so many people.

Conscious classrooms enable young people to be the curator of their own mind, open to learning, actively allowing them to form meaning and purpose for their life, having conscious agency to discern the life they wish to lead. This proactive process allows them to nurture their identity, their internal sense of their authentic self and their role in society, which forms their overall character; built on what they value and put into action in their life.

In conscious classrooms, students experience adults with whom they form life-enhancing relationships, which are based on being accepted and loved for who they are as people. They may exhibit a range of neurodiverse aspects of their personality, but each student will feel valued as a unique human being – which we all are. They will experience classrooms that are calm, purposeful and happy. Learning will be in the context of pro-social, collaborative experiences, in an atmosphere of empowering relationships that foster connection, self-confidence, creativity, critical thinking and curiosity.

Such inclusive classrooms build self-discipline, empathy and self-compassion rather than shame and worthlessness, helping students to choose actively who they want to be in the world – a choice that is made not from the coercion of adults, the biased algorithms of the media or the views of polarised political or social influencers but from the freedom that comes from being educated in a VbE school with its focus on the nurturing of ethical intelligence – an empowering concept that I will explain later. With their focus on awareness, conscious classrooms help children to be the best versions of themselves that they can be, have a strong inner moral compass and be active agents of their own destiny.

Now, before I write more about conscious classrooms and their transformational properties, I think you may find it helpful to ask yourself a question, that is the title of this chapter, that I remember being asked to consider as a young teacher. If you are not a teacher, I'm sure you will still have some strong views based on your own experience. The question for you is, "What is your ideal classroom?"

You may care to consider what it would look like in terms of how the space is used, the seating, desks, tables, equipment, displays, lighting and other furniture. What are the students like in terms of their attitudes and behaviour? How would you describe the relationships between adults and students? Is it an inclusive classroom, where all – no matter their religion, ethnicity, disability, neurodiversity or other distinguishing factors – are welcomed for who they are? Is your classroom a fixed space, or have you redefined how children should be educated today? I am sure that because of AI technology and other developments in society, there will be a shift in the schooling system that will herald huge changes in the way children are educated. However, in this book, I will assume that the current systems of educating young people in schools will remain for the immediate future.

I wish I were with you so that we could talk together about what you consider your ideal classroom and your reasons why. You may be thinking that your ideal classroom is not possible in practice because the realities of life and the current system would not allow you to have your ideal classroom. Yes, I agree, some things may be outside of your control, but you will be amazed about how much is within your sphere of influence. If you are a leader in a school or are responsible for a group of schools, then you will have a great deal of influence to create classrooms that really do release the potential of each student: to find their meaning and purpose in life and chose who they want to be and the way they are going to live in the world. Though, as my own research has shown, the key for a wonder-making conscious classroom is YOU.

As you engage with my thoughts, please hang on to your notion of an ideal classroom, considering if what I share with you will support you as the architect of your ideal classroom.

Finally, as I draw this chapter to its conclusion, may I ask you to revisit the key questions and one more as well?

- What do you remember about your personal classroom experiences?
- Who are you?
- Who have you chosen to be in the world?

- What is your ideal classroom?
- What can you do immediately to begin creating your ideal classroom?

Congratulations! You're on your way to creating a conscious classroom.

In Chapter 2, I'll give you some interesting background and insights into why consciousness-enhancing Values-based Education should be considered such a relevant and appropriate way of educating young people and, importantly, why a transformed educational system, and its schools and settings, should adopt VbE if humanity is to flourish on our planet. I'll also provide you with a practical guide to take you through the process of creating a conscious school and classrooms.

2

My journey to understanding how to enhance consciousness

Welcome to Chapter 2. I hope the previous chapter has filled you with a sense of your own courageous agency, as someone who is a real hero and has the capacity and desire to work towards having an ideal classroom. Yes, believe me when I say that you are a hero, because you send messages to the future. The interactions and the influence you have all leave their mark on your students, and your impact can never be minimised.

In this chapter, my aim is to share with you relevant aspects of my own professional journey that have given me the passion, energy and evidence to share the incredible insights I have gained through visiting thousands of schools and listening to the voices of school leaders, colleague teachers and support staff in many countries.

What I promote, and passionately recommend to you, is drawn from a collective wisdom which I now have the privilege to share with you. This is summarised in a VbE Guide that I am

DOI: 10.4324/9781003681144-2

delighted to share with you in Chapter 3. In sharing my road to West Kidlington School and the VbE Guide, I want to acknowledge the wisdom and insights of the colleagues who supported me and showed total trust in me. They include Linda Heppenstall (values curriculum lead), Bob Laines (chair of governors) and members of the local community of West Kidlington School.

Let's now delve deeply into how conscious schools and their classrooms enhance consciousness by enabling students to be more aware of themselves, others and their environment. I have found the method to do this is through a form of holistic education known globally as Values-based Education (VbE), which I began to research and pioneer in the 1990s.

The genesis of the conscious classroom

In 1993, a transformational form of values education, later known as Values-based Education, was conceived and implemented at a community primary and nursery school in Oxfordshire, UK. It was developed as an integral and explicit part of the school's curriculum (totality of student experiences) and pedagogy (methods and practice of teaching), as a method for educating students in positive human values such as trust, humility, compassion, joy, hope and love. Over a period of seven years, its impact on the quality of teaching and learning was monitored and evaluated as the research subject of my doctoral thesis at Oxford University (Hawkes, 2005). The research was supervised by Professor Richard Pring, the renowned moral philosopher, who was the director of the University's Education Department between 1989 and 2003.

Subsequently, VbE has been recognised throughout the world as an effective model for embedding quality education, including ethical and character education. West Kidlington School's transformational and unique pedagogy transformed the life, work and culture of the school and its community, having a significant lasting impact on both adults and children.

What is VbE?

I define Values-based Education as a transformative practical philosophy and pedagogy of education, which focuses on the wellbeing and holistic education of young people. It is based on learning about and reflecting upon an ethical vocabulary, enabling young people to make informed moral choices about who they want to be in the world.

Simply put, VbE is an umbrella term for structures, routines and activities in schools, underpinning everything the school does, empowering students to understand themselves, others and the world, so that they can make informed life choices based on the principles (values) that guide their thinking and behaviour.

My VbE journey

I hope you will find this next section both fascinating and revealing, as it will help you to understand where my passion, total commitment and belief in the transformational power of VbE came from. I think that our life stories are so important, as they define who we are and our legacy. As you reflected on your own life journey, you will have become aware of all the influences that have formed the person you are today.

For as long as I can remember, I have been passionate about how children best learn and how schools can create an environment and pedagogy that allows all to flourish as human beings. I love my vocation as a teacher; it formed my meaning and purpose in life. At the age of 27, I was appointed as headteacher of Braywood School, a small English rural school near Windsor in the UK. I was fascinated to understand why children learn and behave in the way that they do; how crucial good relationships are in creating an environment for learning to take place. I saw how important it is that home and school co-operate in harmony together. I wrote an M.Ed. thesis at Reading University, UK, on this important topic (Hawkes, 1977).

Two years later I was promoted to be the headteacher of The Palmer School, a large urban school in Wokingham, UK, where I remained for six very happy years. During this period, I built on my previous experience as a headteacher, working with colleagues to create a school where students were excited to learn about the world. My educational vision was to create a school that gave students meaning and purpose for their lives: learning experiences that would form their understanding of themselves and the world, a teaching environment that released the creative dynamic of all who worked in the school. My reputation as an educator and school leader spread; in 1983 I was encouraged by county officials to take my knowledge and experience to be a schools' county education adviser for Buckinghamshire, a large county in England. Five years later, I was promoted to be the county principal adviser of the Isle of Wight Education Service, having responsibility for supporting the educational development of its schools.

It was during this period as a schools' adviser in the late 1980s that I had two significant personal experiences. The first involved taking a party of teachers to Israel for a study visit. At the time I had a wide range of responsibilities, which included the middle years of schooling (8–12), environmental education and religious education. In Israel, we visited Yad Vashem, the memorial to the Holocaust, and I was drawn to visit the place where the children who were murdered by the Nazis are remembered. I entered what seemed to be a dark cave. My eyes became accustomed to the light. I became aware of what appeared at first sight to be hundreds of candles – yet there were only a few. Their radiant light was being reflected on glass panels to create a visual impression that I can only describe as deeply spiritual. As I mindfully walked through the memorial, the only noticeable sound was that of a lone voice of a person who was carefully and respectfully reciting the names of the children who had been murdered by the Nazi regime. The simplicity, power and horror of this experience touched me deeply. When I emerged from the darkness into the sunlight, I was aware of tears smarting my eyes. In a few minutes of deep reflection, I had an overwhelming realisation that my future career must be spent helping people, especially children, to understand and appreciate the common humanity, value and dignity of all people. An education was needed that would transform human consciousness so that atrocities, such as in a holocaust, would not be repeated. Current world events give ample evidence of the need for such education.

The second experience was not such a dramatic, deeply personal event but happened over an extended period. As I visited numerous schools as an education adviser, I was becoming aware that I was observing increasing numbers of children with behaviours that showed that they lacked a knowledge and understanding of words such as respect, empathy, caring, responsibility, love, trust and peace. Teachers were asking for courses to be arranged for them to help them manage classroom organisation and particularly student behaviour.

Some schools were harmonious with few problems connected with student behaviour. These schools were ones that had a culture that focused on the individual needs of students, having a pedagogy built on giving children time and space to explore first-hand experiences. These autonomous schools had outstanding relational cultures but were coming under increasing government pressures to change their methodology to cover the detailed requirements of the newly introduced National Curriculum (National Curriculum, 1989), school league tables and a national Inspection Service (Ofsted, 1992). By 1991, schools were experiencing a national focus on basic literacy and numeracy. This situation made me wonder what I should do to keep my meaning and purpose alive as an educator.

A defining moment for me came in 1992. I recall giving a talk about good educational practices to a large group of teachers at a conference on the Isle of Wight. I thought I was engaging and inspiring the audience, until I noticed someone sitting at the back of the room who seemed totally disengaged from my presentation. I used all my teaching skills to engage the person who had her arms folded and who I imagined was tutting disapproval under her breath. In my mind, a part of me was curious about this situation and another was disturbed. Although I continued with the talk, my internal world was chaotic. I became critical of myself, wondering why I couldn't inspire the person. My internal dialogue was imagining what the person was thinking. Perhaps she was thinking, "If he really knew what he was talking about, then he would go and do it, not just talk to us about it."

Such thoughts had a profound 'road to Damascus' effect on me. At the end of the presentation, which I'm pleased to tell you was warmly received, I returned to my office at County Hall, reflected for a few minutes, and then decided to resign my senior leadership position and return to a school headship – to put my thoughts and words about education for the future into action. In other words, to put into practice what I was talking about to teachers and gain the evidence to show that it was effective and worked!

This sudden, some said reckless, decision dramatically changed my career path; some colleagues remarked to me that I was demoting myself (how wrong they turned out to be), as I returned to a headship, becoming the headteacher of West Kidlington School, a large urban school in Oxfordshire, UK. For the next seven years, I worked closely with exceptionally talented colleagues and a receptive school community to introduce Values-based Education as the basis of the school's educational philosophy. I wanted the school's work to be academically recognised as having an impact on improving the quality of education, so I applied to be a part-time doctoral student at Oxford University. Professor Richard Pring became my supervisor, and Professor Mark Halstead was asked by the university to be an external supervisor. This latter provision was to ensure that by researching the effects of education in my own school, I wasn't compromising the ethics of the research. Professor Halstead suggested that I also conduct research in a school that would form a comparative case study.

The vacancy in the Times Educational Supplement for a headteacher at West Kidlington School had particularly caught my eye because, in small print, it had said, "School just burnt down!" I was curious and was drawn to finding out more. In England there is a fireworks festival called Bonfire Night, which, on the 5th of November, remembers the failed attempt by Guy Fawkes to blow up the Houses of Parliament in London. So, it was on one of these nights that some fireworks had been put through the door of the school, which set the building ablaze.

The single-story building burned quickly. The fire brigade was only able to save a small part of the building, the school's nursery for the youngest students. The teachers shared with me their trauma when they heard that their precious school and its resources had been destroyed. The headteacher, Paul Canterbury, a highly respected headteacher who was nearing the end of his career, decided to retire following this heart-breaking event.

The home of Values-based Education

On taking up my appointment as headteacher of West Kidlington School, a series of temporary buildings were erected on the school field whilst the new school was being built. The local education authority, Oxfordshire County Council, designed a building that was architecturally distinctive with spaces that provided for the learning needs of the students. The building and the values pedagogy of the school are described in Frances Farrer's insightful book about the school, entitled *A Quiet Revolution* (Rider, 2000).

The school was like the mythical story of the phoenix rising from the ashes. As the building took its form, so did the school's philosophy of Values-based Education. The governing body of the school gave me its full support to underpin every aspect of the school's life and work with a set of universal positive human values, such as respect, trust, justice, humility, quality and happiness. It was, and still is, my conviction that children yearn, albeit unconsciously, to be inducted into enhancing values that can guide their thinking and behaviour, so that they can become the best possible versions of themselves. I thought deeply about how my style of leadership would empower each member of the school's community. For instance, I ensured that adults understood that in the school there was only a hierarchy of roles, never of relationships. This meant that all colleagues, teaching and support, knew what role they played in the structure of the school but felt equally valued as human beings. This reflected my commitment to the value of dignity: the inherent worth of all human beings.

The staff (teaching and support colleagues) embraced the values vocabulary, which was not imposed but was the result of a community consultation. The community was asked to decide what dispositions (described as values) it wanted their children to develop during their time at the school. This gave rise to a core set of twenty-two values. Each was the subject of a monthly in-depth study over a two-year cycle. During their six years at the school, students considered a value three times in experiential lessons, each time at a greater depth.

The monthly value was introduced in an assembly that enabled students to understand its meaning. Assemblies were held separately for children 3–5, 5–7 and 7–11 years of age to ensure that the subject material that was used was appropriate to the children's level of understanding. A great deal of thought was given to ensure that assemblies were very special times in the school day. Thought was given to creating a reflective ambience in the room through appropriate calming music and visual displays. Lighting was used to enhance a creative or spiritual atmosphere, especially during the telling of stories or the acting out of a student-led piece of drama. Adults sat with the students, modelling the behaviour they were expecting the children to assume. Students were encouraged to be self-led, so no adult was expected to speak with children to remind them about appropriate behaviour. As the work became embedded in the culture of the school, the students were so proud that adults treated them with respect and understanding.

A central feature of the assemblies was the opportunity to develop reflective practices. In 1993, this was at the time before mindfulness had entered our vocabulary and practice. The school wanted students to be able to inwardly reflect about themselves, their attitudes and behaviour and to consider the learning that they were experiencing. It aimed to support the development of their emotional intelligence, their ability to visualise scenes and events sensitively and creatively on the screen of their minds. Reflection also became a key feature of lessons, with brain breaks being used to give time for a student to be inwardly reflective about what they were learning and how they were responding to what they were learning. I was convinced that helping children to reflect about values and their practical application during assemblies and lessons would give them the skills to gradually gain greater personal control (*self-regulation*) of their inner world of thoughts, feelings, sensations and emotions.

In 1997, the national school inspection service Ofsted validated this in their report of the school, in which was written:

> Spiritual, moral, social and cultural development is an outstanding feature of the school. The consistent and successful implementation of the school's values policy, enhanced by the excellent role models provided by staff and adult helpers, contributes significantly to standards and results in high quality relationships and excellent pupil behaviour.
>
> (Ofsted, 1997)

Values-based assemblies became a feature of the school which many visitors asked to witness. One such visitor was Professor Lovat, from Newcastle University in Australia. He and his research team were looking to support the introduction of values education across Australian schools – a federal initiative. He suggested that the work of West Kidlington School be used as a 'gold standard' that could act as a model of good practice in Australian schools. This decision resulted in my making several visits to Australia to support its national programme. Professor Lovat and colleagues later produced a research report, which validated my own research at Oxford University, across a much larger sample of schools (Lovat et al, 2009).

May I deviate from my story? I recently interviewed Professor Lovat as part of a podcast series that I host on major Internet platforms called Noble Conversations. These are inspiring conversations with people who are living their values and having an impact, often globally. During the interview, Terry was reflecting about his research based on 400 schools in Australia that were implementing Values-based Education. He said:

> What our research validated was that when values are featured in the curriculum, there is greater consciousness and adherence to values such as trust, care etc. Second, there are greater social wellbeing factors: students and staff are happier because of higher levels of mutual trust. Lastly, students actually work more effectively in a values-based school environment.

Terry went on to emphasise that,

> The Jury is *in* about what works in the learning environment. What Pythagoras said, two and a half thousand years ago, is as true now as it was then. Students learn best in a congenial and positive environment. They need to know what the education is for, and they need to feel safe and secure – they

> need to feel cared for. They need also meaningful engagement, when their imagination (imaginative cognition) is linked to learning. There's no real knowing until the imagination is activated. They will know how to spell Napoleon and learn about his campaigns, if that matters to them; if it doesn't, they can swat up for a test but will soon forget because no real learning has taken place. Why can't we get this message over to politicians and policy makers?

I am indebted to Terry for his scholarship, which is endorsed by cognitive neuroscientists, such as Professor Mark Williams in Australia.

To continue my journey: Following the introduction and clarification of a monthly value in an assembly, teachers would revisit the value in the context of an experiential lesson, embedding learning at an age- and stage-appropriate level of understanding. As well as the explicit teaching about values, the staff used the whole of the vocabulary in an implicit way, for instance, in the way that they would talk and interact with students. As students entered the classroom, they might say, "Thank you for coming in so respectfully," or, "Thank you Sameer and Jacob for the way you were co-operating in your game on the playground. As I watched you, I thought you showed each other so much respect." As the staff used and modelled the vocabulary in their daily interactions, so did the children. Parents shared with teachers that the understanding of the values words was helping their family to live more harmoniously. A parent remarked to me that the values had affected the way she spoke and responded to her children.

As the values-based philosophy developed, teacher Linda Heppenstall became the curriculum leader for values education in the school. Her outstanding commitment, along with all members of staff, led to a consistency of good practice that created a unique culture that was described as calm, purposeful and happy in *A Quiet Revolution* (Rider, 2000).

West Kidlington became known as a 'no shouting school', as the school demonstrated that inappropriate shouting and shaming cannot be tolerated in a school that teaches about values such as respect. Staff soon noticed the positive effect that the values were having in encouraging good student behaviour and a positive attitude to learning. The reputation of the school drew the attention of writers, such as Matthieu Ricard, well known for his book *Happiness*, who wrote about the school's methods and their impact in his international bestseller *Altruism* (Atlantic Books, 2015).

It had also led to Linda Heppenstall and me being invited to UNICEF headquarters in New York in 1996 to be part of the team that founded the international programme Living Values Education. The UNICEF leader of the Early Years Cluster, the inspiring Cyril Dalais, saw the potential of values education to help challenging global issues, such as the education of girls. Diane Tillman (who authored the Living Values series of resource books), Lynn Henshall (secretary of Living Values Education in the British Isles) and a team of global educators made up the founding group, who profoundly influenced my own thinking and development.

The transformational elements of Values-based Education

Bridget Knight, a colleague teaching at a local school, was curious about what she had heard about the transformational curriculum at West Kidlington. She asked to visit the school to observe an assembly and lessons. Later she remarked that the values dynamic of the school was outstanding: simple yet profound in its impact on children as people and the quality of their learning. Bridget went on to be the head of a values-based school and then led the development of values-based education as a senior adviser for the county of Herefordshire. She returned to a headship at Eardisley Church of England Primary School – an outstanding VbE school. She is now CEO of Values-based Education, which is the educational arm of a charity I formed called the International Values-based Education Trust, commonly known as the IVET Foundation. Bridget has a deep and profound understanding about values and their impact in our lives. In VbE's Early Years Audit tool, she wrote about what values are and what they do. Here are her words:

> To *value* something is to consider it with respect to worth, excellence, usefulness or importance, so we use values like kindness, respect and hope to see, reason and eventually become. They bring a universal objectivity with them: 'care' means caring for me, for you, for the world . . . it can apply to everything. When we start noticing values in different places, we start to build a jigsaw in our brain . . . our brains like having puzzles to solve . . . then we start to find meaning, and when we start to find meaning, we start to care . . . this changes our outlook and behaviours. The *vocabulary of values* develops ethical habits, and patterns of thinking, speaking and behaving, that make for successful learning and living. Explicitly naming and living by a values-based vision breathes those values into life. In so doing, we transform outlook, attitudes and prospects for every single learner.

MIRACLE

Jane thought that the acronym MIRACLE (that which causes wonder) provided a memorable way for educators to remember the key elements of VbE, which are introduced simultaneously. These are:

- **Modelling** (the thinking and behaviour of adults and students),
- **Inner curriculum** (enabling the inner world of the student, and staff, to be self-led),
- **Relationships** (understanding the importance of forming appropriate relationships),
- **Atmosphere** (the ethos, culture and character of the school, expressed in the school's routines, structures, display and ambience),
- **Curriculum** (the development of an explicit VbE curriculum and its links to the wider curriculum),
- **Leadership** (the understanding, commitment to leading and developing a values-based school),
- **Ethical vocabulary** (the positive values words).

In 2013, I captured the uniqueness of the VbE methods in my book *From My Heart: Transforming Lives Through Values* (Independent Thinking Press, 2013). The book is a celebration of schools that are explicitly values based. It also gives information about how to create a values-based school. In 2018, I thought that the transformational elements of VbE's Inner Curriculum required a book of their own. Consequently, Jane and I co-wrote *The Inner Curriculum: How to Nourish Wellbeing, Resilience and Self-Leadership* (John Catt Educational, 2018). In this book, we drew on insights from the world of psychotherapy, particularly the work of Dr Richard Schwartz and his book on internal family systems (IFS) therapy (Guilford Press, 1995). IFS emphasises the essence of a human being, which he describes as Self. Jane was the first to notice that much of VbE's success as an educational philosophy is because it makes it safe for our authentic Self in us to be fully present. I now describe this as VbE's secret ingredient!

Values-based Education is transformational

If Values-based Education is transformational, then what does it transform? I believe it transforms classrooms and schools by raising consciousness, our awareness of ourselves as thinking, feeling people. To raise consciousness, VbE nourishes the essential characteristics of human beings, which I see as positive and life affirming. These include co-operation, love, peace, altruism, equality and justice – expressed as virtues (values that are lived). Nurturing this essence in children helps them to take control of their feelings, which may spring from holding onto limiting values, such as jealousy (unpleasant suspicion), greed (selfish desire) or envy (discontented longing). Professor Mark Williams, the cognitive neuroscientist, has told me that the positive characteristics of human beings are what has made our species so successful – we can connect with each other through them. You can read about Mark's insights in his wonderful book *The Connected Species* (Rowman & Littlefield, 2023).

Thus, enriching a child's vocabulary with one that is ethical, based on positive human values, nurtures what I describe as ethical intelligence. This intelligence, which includes emotional intelligence, I define as the ability to ethically self-regulate and be the leader of one's own behaviour, based on this essential energy which nourishes consciousness. The potential impact of ethical intelligence, if it were both at the core of the school curriculum and the key outcome of education, would be life-enhancing – truly transformational. I believe that there would be a paradigm shift in the way that humans think about what it means to be human and how people should relate to each other locally and globally if ethical leadership were the priority for character development. Where do we start? In creating conscious classrooms!

Now let's be more practical, as I sense you would like more information about how you create your conscious school and classrooms, underpinned by the principles of VbE. For this purpose, you will see that I have created a guide in Chapter 3, a pathway with a structured process that will support you as a teacher and/or school leader as you create conscious classrooms.

Finally, some thoughts for you explore . . .

I must admit that I felt quite emotional writing this chapter, as I have shared with you the transformational aspects of my personal journey, which have led me to arrive at the realisation that humanity could become more altruistically conscious if children were to be educated in conscious classrooms.

- Were there aspects of my journey that touched your heart or challenged your thinking?
- What ideas are you taking away with you?
- What will you do differently?

3

The Guide to creating a conscious school and classrooms

I think it is so important that you fully understand that the Guide that I am going to share with you is firmly rooted in my personal experience and research as the headteacher of the first explicitly values-based school in the UK.

It may be helpful if I remind you that the foundation of a conscious classroom is Values-based Education (VbE). This assertion is drawn from the evidence from ground-breaking research conducted by me at Oxford University in the UK and Professor Terry Lovat at Newcastle University in Australia, supported by wide-ranging evidence from VbE schools globally (Hawkes, 2005; Lovat et al, 2009). The evidence supports my assertion that conscious classrooms are created in educational settings that have embraced a successful, holistic, educational philosophy, namely Values-based Education.

 DOI: 10.4324/9781003681144-3

What is VbE?

As I shared with you in the previous chapter, Values-based Education is a practical, transformative philosophy of education which focuses on the wellbeing, ethical self-leadership and holistic education of young people. It is based on learning about and reflecting upon an ethical vocabulary (values consciousness), enabling students to make informed moral choices about who they want to be in the world.

The outcome of VbE is the fostering of agency (the ability to act) across a range of human intelligences, including intra- and inter-personal, emotional, critical, creative, kinaesthetic, environmental and ethical-moral.

"Wow!" I sense you are saying, "What does all that mean, Neil?" Simply put, it means that by considering, experiencing, understanding and practising a range of human values, such as respect, trust and courage, students will act from an understanding of values as they respond to real-life situations. In other words, they will develop their character by understanding themselves; being aware of the needs of others and the environment; being able to distinguish truth from fiction; having creative, intuitive imagination; being aware and caring for their bodies. By nurturing this heightened consciousness, students will gain moral agency, which is the ability to ethically self-regulate their thinking and behaviour. Can you imagine a world led by leaders who have these capabilities and aspects of character? It's my dream, and I hope it will be yours too!

The Guide will support you as you create your conscious school and classrooms, underpinned by Values-based Education. It is written in the knowledge that the success of VbE is based on research evidence that confirms that students' awareness of values, agency, behaviour and academic diligence will be enhanced if they are in a learning environment that gives them access to, and the living of, an ethical-moral vocabulary; a vocabulary based on enhancing human values, such as dignity, respect, compassion, justice and integrity. This means that when adults have introduced a community-agreed set of values, the adults agree to model the values to students who will then learn about the values experientially. This Guide provides the basic, essential, background knowledge of VbE, which I invite you to implement. For a more comprehensive account, please consult *From My Heart, Transforming Lives Through Values* (Independent Thinking Press, 2013); also there are videos and comprehensive information on valuesbasededucation.com that can be used with your school community.

Aims of VbE

It is important to appreciate that Values-based Education aims to underpin every aspect of the life and work of school communities, colleges and other settings, including the home, so that all settings are authentically values based and thereby more conscious about what they do and why. The term *values-based* implies that all aspects of life, both personal and professional, are founded on the way that positive, human values are used as principles to guide our thinking and subsequent behaviour. This highly practical, educational philosophy is transformational, in that it drives personal and cultural change, based on dignity (the inherent worth of each of us), equity (being fair and just) and respect (due regard for the feelings, wishes and rights of others) for all. It is challenging, as it calls on us to ask what we can give to life, as opposed to what can we take from life. It promotes a way of being that values the self, others and the environment. VbE's impact is wide ranging and comprehensive, as it develops an awareness of the importance of understanding the central role that values play in our lives. Learning about and living a normative set of values nurtures what I describe as ethical intelligence, the ability to ethically self-regulate our behaviour. Other benefits include increased *academic diligence*; *enhanced relational trust*; and the *promotion of self, other and environmental awareness*. It encourages *communicative competence*, gives us a *moral compass* and nurtures *agency*, which I have described as *self-leadership*.

I believe that self-leadership, which I describe in Chapter 4, is the amazing gift of VbE. The VbE school atmosphere nurtures this quality in students because it allows them to be their authentic selves, free to express their true natural essence. The conscious classroom creates the safe space where each person is welcomed for who they are. The conscious classroom may be likened to a field of values, where we can play, learn, and explore who we are becoming and choose to be in the world.

As an aside, in May 2023, I spoke at the United Nations in Geneva about Values-based Leadership being based on ethical self-leadership: the overarching aspect of character that leaders at all levels in society need to have if our world is to flourish. I argued passionately that to solve the complex issues that humanity faces, we need values-based leadership, grounded in ethics. Students in values-based classrooms begin the process of developing the capacity to be ethical leaders, by learning to ethically self-regulate their behaviour.

VbE is profound in its outcomes and, I would argue, should be adopted by all schools worldwide. However, some do not adopt it because they haven't heard of it or have a lack of understanding about what constitutes quality education that is relevant for young people today. To create conscious classrooms requires enlightened, determined leadership and a consistent and agreed approach to humane teaching and learning by *all* staff.

VbE has seven core components expressed in the acronym MIRACLE

1. Authentic **modelling** by adults of positive values.
2. The **Inner Curriculum**, creating awareness of our thoughts, feelings and emotions.
3. Nurturing caring, respectful, inclusive **relationships**.
4. The creation of a calm, purposeful and happy VbE **atmosphere**, both physical and emotional.
5. The development of an explicit VbE **curriculum** and its links to the wider curriculum.
6. The development of quality values-led **leadership**.
7. The comprehensive development of an **ethical vocabulary**, which nurtures ethical intelligence and self-leadership.

Twelve steps to developing a values-based school

This VbE Guide has become an inspiration for classrooms and schools worldwide, and is founded on the original, highly successful, innovative work at West Kidlington School in Oxfordshire, UK. The school was the first school that was explicitly values-based in the way this Guide describes. The process is summarised in this diagram:

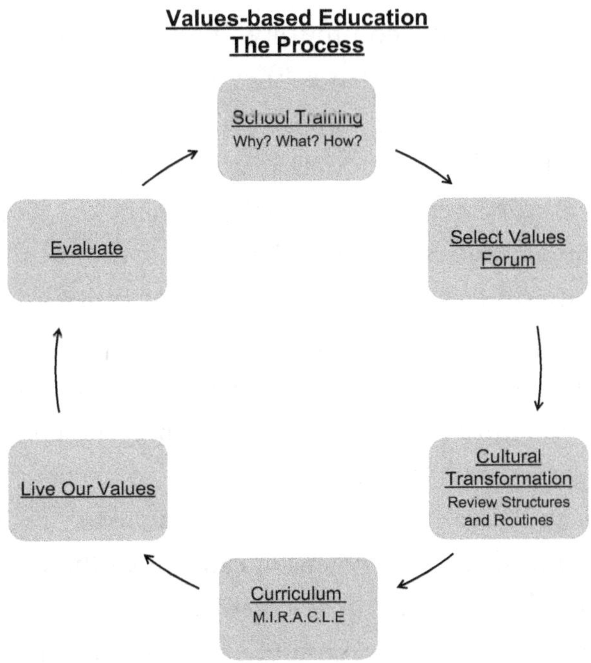

FIGURE 3.1 Values-based Education process

I recommend that you follow The Guide's key steps.

Step 1. Why do you want to introduce VbE?

First, be clear about why you want to develop VbE in your school and become a conscious school. Look at valuesbasededucation.com and neilhawkes.org to ensure that you understand what VbE is and how you can embed it in your school. It is imperative that the leadership of the school be *fully committed* to the development of a values-based school culture. That means being prepared to act as role models for VbE. Have you seen a VbE school, read about one or considered the research evidence for introducing VbE?

I have found that values-based leaders have thought about their own core values that drive their behaviour. They are authentic and regularly communicate their values to colleagues and the wider school community. They consider themselves ethically self-led leaders; that is, they regulate their own behaviour based on enhancing values such as compassion, integrity and trust. They are role models as values-based leaders.

Leaders empower and encourage others to develop their own potential. Values-based leadership informs all the school's actions, provision and decision-making. At times it is demanding, requiring a courageous and principled stance. The headteacher/principal is key, because he/she is the principal architect of the school's purpose and vision, affirming the school's values. I have observed that having the capacity to access their internal world and dream (use creative imagination) brings transformational positive energy (inspiration) into the formation of a VbE school – a prime characteristic of an altruistic leader. This, coupled with the seemingly endless capacity to access their own reservoir of uncontaminated self-energy, enables the leader(s) to remain stable and focused on an educational context of incomparable complexity and challenge. It is through their commitment, drive, care and ability to inspire others that the leader creates a sustainable school culture based on VbE, which has the active support of all members of staff, ensuring consistency of practice across all aspects of school life. A VbE school encourages all members of the school, both adults and children, to be seen as ethical leaders, taking personal responsibility for their thoughts and behaviour and sustaining an ethical vocabulary.

Next, decide who will be the lead in the school for the introduction of VbE. Or will a mix of people take responsibility for VbE's development from both the school and its community? Are you prepared to invest the necessary time, energy and resources for its successful adoption?

Then, think about timescale for implementation, success criteria, monitoring and evaluation. Help colleagues to realise that VbE is about school cultural transformation, challenging personal assumptions and mindsets about the nature of education and schooling. This is important, as values education is a community activity and not an imposition from one person.

I suggest that, with their full agreement, there is time for staff to discuss their personal values and their perception of current and desired values of the school. This creates opportunity for staff to think about the values that guide their thinking and behaviour. Will the school's institutional values be in synergy with the values of staff members? It is vital that all members of staff openly agree to be the role models of the school's chosen values.

Importantly, ensure that you think about and review your current culture for teaching and learning, relationships, level of co-operation among staff and level of cultural entropy (aspects of the school's culture, routines and structures that work against its being values-based). Ask: how does our school currently impart values to students? What are these values? Are they taught implicitly or explicitly? What do we hope will be the benefits of being a values-based school?

Each school is unique; therefore, the way you introduce values into your school will be dependent on your school's context and the needs of your students. This will include an understanding of the needs of the adults, too! Effective care of staff is a fundamental principle of Values-based Education. Considering how your school meets the needs of staff and students is a crucial aspect and will draw out issues concerning the valuing of all students, showing students respect and being authentic as a person. Students soon spot inconsistencies between what teachers say and what they do. A good sense of fun and humour is also a prerequisite.

Step 2. Select your school's values

This part of The Guide is crucial in successfully introducing VbE.

Ideally, the whole school community (staff, students, parents and community representatives) will be involved in shaping a values-based education policy. A process of values understanding/identification takes place involving the school's community. A meeting/forum is set up to facilitate this process. The forum will propose that the school adopt universal, positive, human values such as respect, honesty, justice, compassion, trust, equality, freedom and co-operation.

I suggest that the school's values be chosen through a careful process that involves thinking about what qualities (values) the school will encourage students to develop as their compass for life. During the selection process, it is important that most people agree on the values chosen. This can be done by a simple show of hands for each of the proposed values. This will avoid a value being selected that could be considered divisive.

The list of values suggested by the forum is then circulated to all parents and stakeholders for consultation and endorsement so that all are aware of the values that have been proposed and general agreement achieved. This is the most effective way of engaging the community in the values process. In secondary schools, it is imperative that students be actively involved in the selection process of values.

Step 3. Implementation of the school's values

Values-based Education develops what I have called *ethical intelligence*, which is the guide to the self-regulation of students' thinking and subsequent behaviour. This capacity is nurtured when young people are introduced to an *ethical vocabulary* based on positive values words (such as respect, honesty and co-operation).

The implementation model that I recommend for primary/ elementary schools has twenty-two values, introduced over a two-year cycle: one value being the focus for each month except in the long holiday break. Implicitly the school staff use these values words when talking with students and model them. I believe that such a vocabulary, if adopted at national level, can be the basis of a transformational common universal narrative, bringing peace to the world. In secondary schools, which build on the work of their primary feeder schools, you may decide to have fewer values but have supplementary values that are the focus for the development of character traits such as fairness, perseverance, altruism and integrity.

Serving the school community on voluntary projects gives opportunities for students to live the values and develop character traits. By the time students leave secondary school, they will have developed what I term *Personal Holistic Competence* (PHC), which is the ability to deal with the complexity of life in an ethical and empathetic manner whilst maintaining personal integrity and wellbeing. Students demonstrate that they have the capacity to be *ethical leaders*. I recommend that *ethical leadership* be central to your curriculum and become its main outcome. Our world desperately needs all of us to be ethical leaders if we are to solve the complex issues that face humanity.

Step 4. Deciding principles for adults

In the light of the values identified, the school decides the principles that will guide the way adults behave. Elements will be discussed to determine these such as:

- How all adults will care for their mental wellbeing and health and be mutually supportive.
- How adults will be consistent in their behaviour, leading to consistency of behaviour by all members of staff (teaching and non-teaching), so students will experience the same care and respect from all members of staff.
- The emotional, intellectual, physical, moral and spiritual needs of the students will be considered to ensure that the curriculum is holistic, that it nurtures all aspects of the student.
- The way students will be treated, in terms of the school's relational (behaviour) policy: sanctions and rewards.

Step 5. Role models

Adults in the school must be willing to commit themselves to work towards being role models for Values-based Education. Its success, in terms of improved standards and school ethos, will only come about if the school headteacher/principal and all staff (teaching and support staff) understand that it is primarily through their behaviour in modelling the values that sustainable improvements will develop in the school.

The adults therefore identify and agree positive behaviours that will model the values, such as remaining calm when dealing with challenging student behaviour, investing time in really getting to know their students, helping students to sense and shape their future by finding meaning and purpose for what they do and being respectful at all times.

Such an agreement may be recorded in job descriptions and form part of performance management.

Step 6. School culture

There should be a review of the school's culture, as expressed in routines and structures – such as considering how parents are welcomed, school signage, state of the buildings and grounds, cleanliness, sports days, concerts, parents' meeting and health matters. This will reveal where there is consistency, or not, with the values-based education policy.

Be curious about why the school has ways of doing things. Are they still relevant? Are they consistent with the school's values?

Step 7. The Inner Curriculum and reflection

In Chapter 4, I will explain, in some depth, the importance of being aware of the Inner Curriculum (especially your own), the internal realm of thoughts, feelings and emotions. The Inner Curriculum is an invaluable aspect, missing in many schools.

A key aspect of the Inner Curriculum is the skill of reflection (sitting silently and focusing mental energy). Reflection nurtures greater self-regulation, emotional balance, better relationships and responding appropriately to others, which will lead to values-based behaviour and more student agency in their learning. Time needs to be devoted to understanding and training this important skill, as in many schools it will be seen as something outside of the normal work of the school and only linked to faith communities.

I cannot over-emphasise the importance of this skill that has the backing of scientific research – see Dr Dan Siegel's book, *The Mindful Brain* (WW Norton, 2007) – as well as thousands of years of human wisdom.

Step 8. Experiential programme

An experiential programme is established for learning about values, which may include:

- Introducing and deepening the understanding of values in a programme of well-planned assemblies (when all or part of the school meet), one value being highlighted each month or other agreed-upon period of time (e.g. January=Respect); each class teacher (primary schools) preparing one values lesson each month; the value of the month being the subject of a prominent display in the school hall, reception area, headteacher's/principal's office and each classroom; values being an integral part of tutor time and all subject lessons; and a specific area of the (secondary school) curriculum lessons having a values focus as well as a learning intention.
- The language of values used explicitly in all lessons, e.g. "*Well done, you showed great respect to each other,*" "*Thank you for co-operating/caring/being tolerant.*"
- Ensure that reflection is a key component of lessons; "*Let's have a minute of silence so that we can be fully present in our lesson*" or "*Let's pause and check out in a few moments of silence what we are thinking and feeling in this lesson, and what will make our learning more productive*" etc.

- I recommend that students understand the parts and main functions of their brains – age- and stage-appropriate, such as prefrontal cortex, limbic system.
- Students are encouraged to be involved in action teams, using a values perspective to consider school and community issues; How can we improve our break time experience? What can we do to make our learning experience both pleasurable and effective so that we get the most out of school life? How can we encourage our parents and community to be more involved in the life of the school? What can we advise the council to do about litter in the shopping centre?
- Students and staff create classroom values charters that form an agreement about how values are guiding learning and behaviour.
- Regular newsletters are sent to parents, explaining what the value of the month is and how it can be developed at home.

Step 9. Integrate values across the curriculum

Activities are identified that could make a specific contribution to VbE in the curriculum (everything that the school does), e.g. Philosophy for Children (P4C), building learning power, growth mindset, roots of empathy, enquiry-based projects, outdoor learning/forest schools, technology-supported learning, service learning, sports programmes, school concerts/shows and other events.

The range of skills, knowledge, attitudes and understanding to develop from VbE is identified. Of crucial importance is to ensure that the process of developing VbE is well planned (construct an action plan/road map) and that there is continuity and progression in the students' school experience, which is monitored, evaluated and celebrated to keep the process alive and constantly under review. Ensure that VbE is visible in *all* subjects and aspects of the curriculum. The school's values leader or a group of staff, which may include representatives of the student body and community, may lead this process.

Step 10. Values Statement

The school agrees on a *Values Statement* that may be prominently displayed in school and included in the school's prospectus/ website. It may consider working towards achieving the Values-based Education Quality Mark, or even the Enhanced Values-based Education Quality Mark.

Finally, the school community celebrates being a values-based school and continues a process of continuous school improvement.

Step 11. The headteacher/principal as a values and self-led leader

Although I have mentioned the need for the leadership of the school to be committed to VbE, I want to re-emphasise it again in this section of The Guide, as I believe that it is the *most important* aspect.

Effective values-based schools *only* develop if the leader and leadership team of the school see the relevance of VbE as a key driver for creating a world-class school. It is not a soft option, as it demands a lot in terms of personal commitment and drive. This is what Pete Dunmall, head of Fielding Primary School in Ealing, thinks:

> Values enable headteachers to share their vision in a common, consistent vocabulary. Values have helped me provide a framework for decision-making – especially around people – for all the things where there is no guidance and you're

> left on your own. Decisions are taken in the best interest of the organisation and the person themselves. The values vocabulary helps me to explain where the decision has come from. Values provide a framework for reflective thinking, enabling my personal growth and development following every experience: "How might I have managed that better?"

The impact of Values-based Education is profound and permeates the whole school community.

Step 12. Your next steps

If you want to embed VbE in your school and classrooms, it is highly recommended that you set aside a VbE training day, when all teaching and non-teaching staff can attend and be an active part of this process of transformational cultural change. Involvement and ownership are key to the success of VbE.

If you would like support on your values journey, please contact me or other members of the VbE team through values-basededucation.com. We can also give training through Zoom.

And finally, this is what schools are telling me about the impact of VbE:

> At our school, we have implemented VbE as part of our daily curriculum. It is embedded through all our practices and environment, and is interwoven through every element of school life. School assemblies have become a powerful vehicle for teaching about values, raising self-esteem, and developing enthusiasm.
>
> The school has witnessed a decrease in the conflict among students. There is a demonstration of greater empathy, honesty and integrity.

> Students have become more tolerant and co-operative in their interactions, assume responsibility for their own learning and work, and work together co-operatively along with recognition of values in others, as well as in themselves. Democratic classrooms are established, student-teacher relationships have become more trusting, and teachers have become more conscious of scaffolding students to manage their own behaviour or resolve conflicts with others.
>
> We have built our school community on values and have been rewarded with a very happy school atmosphere, well-behaved students, young minds capable of decision-making, a purposeful work ethic, higher quality academic performance and, in our hearts, a better future.
>
> We believe that, when an entire school focuses on values, the impact is greater and more positive.

Before ending this chapter, I would like you to pause and consider these issues:

- For you, what would be your next step in creating a conscious home, classroom or whole school?
- What would be the challenges?
- How would you overcome them?

Now that you understand the practical ways to create conscious classrooms, join me in Chapter 4 for a deep dive into a successful way of expanding consciousness. I think all readers will find it personally and professionally enriching. It will support those of you who are teachers to enable students to be conscious learners.

4

Enhancing consciousness in the classroom by PAUSE to Be

This chapter will help you teach you and your students what I consider an amazing learning super-skill, called PAUSE to Be (P2B).

PAUSE to Be invites us to be still for a while, aware of our internal world of thoughts, feelings and emotions. It gives space for our conscious Self to be present so that we can access the necessary wisdom to guide our thinking and behaviour.

This profound key to deepening and enhancing children's learning, has been part of what I describe as the Inner Curriculum, and I have shared with schools since 2019, mainly in the UK. The Inner Curriculum focuses on the insights that children need in order to understand their internal world of thoughts, feelings and emotions.

At first, PAUSE to Be, which I sometimes shorten to the catchy term P2B, may seem a bit unrelated to your mission as an educator, or you may reject it because you sense it is just a form of mindfulness! As you experience more about it and

DOI: 10.4324/9781003681144-4

delve into its incredible life-enhancing benefits, may I assure you that you will see that it is one of the most important skills for children to learn – dare I say, for you, too.

Many adults have told me that they wished they had learned to PAUSE to Be when they were children. Immersing yourself in this seminal chapter will give you the key information you need to introduce and practise the PAUSE to Be process, which leads to your classroom ethos creating a more conscious space for learning to take place. As adults and students are more aware of their internal worlds, they learn how to regulate them for the benefit of themselves and others.

Introduction

PAUSE to Be is a self-calming and active reflective process that gives students the knowledge and understanding needed for them to regulate their internal world of thoughts, feelings, sensations and emotions. Awareness of the state of our internal world leads to heightened consciousness and greater ability to self-regulate thinking and behaviour.

Neuroscience suggests that the practice has a beneficial effect on the part of our brain called the prefrontal cortex – the seat of our consciousness, strengthening our ability to be in control of our inner world. Incidentally, I recommend that schools ensure that students – age- and stage-appropriate – learn about the parts of their brains and what they do. They are fascinated to know what the parts of their limbic system do, such as the amygdala and hippocampus. In a London school, I remember a boy of about 9 running along a corridor. When I asked him if anything was wrong, he answered that he had just had an amygdala hijack.

Another gift of P2B is co-regulation, that is, a student regulating emotions and behaviours and returning to a calm state because of the conscious calm modelling and support of a connecting adult. Simply put, co-regulation occurs when you, the teacher or teaching assistant, are modelling the behaviour that you wish to see in your classroom. From my classroom observations, made over many years, co-regulation has a profound impact on children's thinking and behaviour. That is why being calm is such an important aspect of good teaching. If you are upset, children will sense that you are, and their behaviour will be impacted by how you are feeling, so I recommend that you take a short period of time out to PAUSE to Be so that you can calm down any strong feelings or emotions that you are experiencing. I witnessed teacher time-out in action when I visited Bannockburn Primary School in London. In this accredited values-based school, the policy for teachers who were feeling triggered by student behaviour was to call for adult support so that they could have a brief time out of the classroom. The headteacher shared with me that the teachers felt that the school was actively looking after their mental wellbeing through this and other caring policies.

In introducing P2B to your students, please be creative and imaginative in the way you use these practical ideas and apply them appropriately to the age and stage of the students. You know what will work with your students. Remember to keep it simple; engage your students in being active in the process of exploring their inner worlds. Keep parents on board, too, so that they can support this work at home and help to maintain their own stable internal worlds. I believe this work will nurture students' character strengths, supporting their mental wellbeing, resilience and the joy of learning in your classroom and school.

May I remind you that the ideas and teaching skills in this chapter sit in the context of your creating a conscious-based classroom, coupled with *all* the key elements I describe in this book. Cherry-picking some ideas or only using them for a limited time will not have the impact that I know can be achieved. Also, please may I remind you that the conscious classroom is not a programme but an holistic pedagogy that covers every aspect of your classroom practice.

Most importantly, please remember that it is your own modelling of this transformational work that will have the greatest impact on your students, so please walk the talk and make what I call The Inner Curriculum a part of your own daily practice. Jane and I wrote a book entitled *The Inner Curriculum: How to Nourish Wellbeing, Resilience and Self-Leadership* (John Catt Educational, 2018), which I recommend to you if you want to broaden your understanding of the elements which create an inner curriculum.

A conscious classroom shines out as one where there is consistent, predictable, adult behaviour: a classroom where students feel safe and secure because of their good relationships with the teacher and other supporting staff. Neurobiology teaches us that our brains are programmed to look for threat and that learning is not stored in the long-term memory unless it is linked to positive emotion. In those that I have visited globally, the most effective teachers and schools place good relationships at the heart of their practice. These are the places where students learn well, feel that they can be their best selves and flourish as people.

Traditionally, schools have a curriculum (knowledge, skills and concepts) that is taught to students. I believe that something crucially important is missing in education if children are to be fully educated and able to thrive in the complex world of the 21st century and beyond.

What is missing is an holistic curriculum that acknowledges and works with the character traits, dispositions and complex nature of a child's personality. This insightful curriculum invites the student to understand and shape their internal world for their own happiness and the benefit of society. The conscious classroom nurtures the student's ability to step back from their emotions, to pause and think about what the wise person would do before taking action. This consciousness-enhancing ability is what I call ethical intelligence, which is our ability to ethically self-regulate our thinking and behaviour. You could call it good common sense. I believe that a focus on developing PAUSE to Be will bring tremendous benefits in the form of improved mental wellbeing and resilience for individuals, better outcomes for schools and a more harmonious society.

What I am encouraging you to do is to embrace PAUSE to Be as a daily part of classroom life. Teachers tell me that it is a practical and enjoyable way to help children to take control of their thoughts and feelings, which makes them happier and the classroom more harmonious. P2B acknowledges and works with the character traits, dispositions and complex nature of a child's personality.

The consequence of this new way of being in the classroom will be that people will be happier and more pro-social in their behaviour, taking the lid off their potential and contributing more productively and sustainably to the future needs of society. Indeed, they will develop self-leadership, which is one of the key attributes and outcomes of being ethically intelligent.

Going deeper

Let's delve a little more deeply into how the conscious classroom teaches students how to be conscious about and in harmonious control of their internal world of thoughts, feelings and emotions. This benign, compassionate control enables them to respond appropriately and altruistically to others, without hurting them or damaging their own sense of Self. Indeed, it supports the development of a strong and secure sense of Self, which develops the disposition of Self-leadership, which sustains wellbeing and resilience.

I use the term Self (see description below) as meaning the innate, peaceful, loving essence of human consciousness, which is an aware, calm, compassionate, healing energy that creates space for the nurturing of wisdom.

Wow! You may need to read the previous paragraph again, as I sense that this may at first reading seem a bit 'way out'. Stay with me! You see, when we experience Self-energy, we are accessing what cognitive neuroscience calls our authentic nature – the real you. I expect you have had those times of 'realness' when you have thought, "I felt my real self today – everything seemed to flow so effortlessly."

I believe that a core objective of education should be to nurture our Self-energy in the context of thinking about and applying human values such as empathy, courage, resilience, dignity, altruism, peace, generosity and justice. Such dispositions, which can become our virtues (values that we live), are often evident when there is a natural disaster or major catastrophe, but sadly these are not universally seen during normal life. I think that conscious classroom schools and other organisations which care deeply about nurturing character development bring such traits into consciousness.

The conscious classroom evolves into a calm, happy, purposeful, relational environment, one that allows the authentic Self to flourish. When our Self-energy is leading our internal world, then we and others have the potential to experience wellbeing, and release our innate creativity and connectedness. Self-energy is contagious, as it makes it safe for this natural quality to emerge in others.

May I invite you to stop reading for a moment and remember a time when you have experienced the deep feeling of being your 'real' Self . . .

Great, wasn't it? I have this sensation when I experience my own P2B times. You see, as humanity shares this simple yet profound wisdom, I hope that it will produce Self-led leaders who embody ethical intelligence. Can you imagine the difference that would make to the peace and flourishing of our world?

What is the Self?

The way I'm using the concept of Self is drawn from the work of Dr Richard Schwartz, based on his transformative theory of psychotherapy called internal family systems (IFS). Based on years of studying IFS and working with Jane (a psychotherapist), there is no doubt in my mind that aspects of IFS give amazing practical tools for developing the conscious classroom. They provide clarity about the nature of children's internal worlds, giving them the tools to help them understand why they feel, think and act in the way that they do.

I hope the following explanation of the term Self will help you understand how I am using this hugely important concept, which encapsulates what it means to be the best person that you can be.

Please be mindful how the words are impacting you. They may trigger you, as they may be in a form of language which seems weird or unfamiliar to you. Please maintain your curiosity and keep an open mind as you explore the words and ideas. At first, I too experienced a degree of cynicism, but experience reassured me that the model of IFS contains profound truths.

To explain in a psychological sense, Self may be understood as your perfect and pure essence, the repository of your innate values. Some spiritual traditions and cultures describe this aspect of us as soul or spirit, whilst others, such as Humanists, may refer to it as the essence of consciousness.

Self is untouched by the less than perfect parts of you, which you have acquired whilst living in the world. Self is your wise, conscious self and, when accessed, is a constant source of healing and wellbeing. Its total absence of disturbance makes this your go-to, still point – a deep enriching experience of peace.

When you PAUSE to Be, being deliberately inwardly reflective, you can take a journey to experience your authentic Self, which compassionately will calm and nurture your internal world. This process brings boundless benefits, enabling you to live your life fuelled by the nourishing power of Self-energy. Self-energy gives us our highest state of consciousness, an inner teacher, fuelled by values such as clarity, creativity, calmness, compassion, courage and connection, which is what our complex world yearns to embrace.

If your students experience P2B, they will begin to discover and experience their Self-energy, which will enhance their experience of themselves, assist their mental wellbeing and help guide their behaviour.

As I mentioned earlier, I am aware that you may be experiencing lots of reactions to the terms and concepts I am sharing. I wish I were with you to answer your questions! As I said earlier, hold on in there because I think your appreciation and understanding of the P2B process will become clear when you experience it practically. So now it's time to be practical.

Let's explore the practice of PAUSE to Be

The PAUSE to Be process gives students a structure to access their P2B powers. You will find that students will really enjoy being given this amazing tool for understanding themselves. I find that the most important point for the teacher is that you must make it a daily practice in your classroom so the routine becomes a habit.

I have chosen the term PAUSE to Be, because I believe that to be the best people we can be, we need to regularly stop and pause to *be*. PAUSE to Be gives us time in our busy and complex lives to take our attention inward, to sense and be aware of the state of our internal world. We discover if it is busy, distressed, disengaged, content, overwhelmed. We check what activity (thought, emotion and sensation) is taking place and what regulation, if any, we need to action. PAUSE helps us to be conscious about our internal world so that we can deliberately adjust and maintain a sense of internal equilibrium. We are then empowered, in an atmosphere of internal calmness, to clarify and shape our thoughts, so that we have the energy of Self-leadership to speak and act from our authentic Self and to truly be ourselves.

As you introduce your class to the acronym PAUSE, I suggest that you help students to make PAUSE to Be a daily habit, as is appropriate to the age and stage of their development. The benefits of the process accrue with regular practice over time. Making it something that you do in the class on a regular basis (at least once a day) will enable your students to have space and time to experience feeling peaceful, and have time to be more aware about what's happening in their internal worlds. By turning their attention inward, students learn to be aware of the nature of their internal world. They learn how to understand it compassionately, which helps them to regulate their thinking and behaviour. An outcome will be that they are likely to experience self-attachment, which is having a secure sense of self, which gives them a profound awareness of wellbeing and helps them to enjoy learning. It also can help in their development of healthy attachments with others.

Understanding PAUSE to Be before teaching it to your class

The acronym PAUSE invites us into an active, sequential process – a wisdom cycle (stop, reflect, act), which gives space and time to explore our inner landscape of thoughts, feelings, sensations and emotions. Each letter of PAUSE helps us to remember each part of the process, as I explain later.

On pausing and being still, we consciously slow and deepen our breath, which calms our internal world and connects us to our innate, inner peacefulness.

Next, we pay attention to what we notice inside, maybe thoughts, tensions, feelings or emotions. We simply breathe, being aware of what we are thinking, hearing and feeling.

We gain an understanding about what we are being invited to know from our inner world, which we can think of as our inner family. By being aware of our thoughts and inner experiences, we have insights into why we are thinking and behaving in a particular way, or what's creating the mood that we are experiencing. We gain a clarity and a deeper understanding of our inner world.

Throughout this process, we are creating more space in our inner system to be filled with Self-energy (consciousness), which is our innate values 'treasure chest', including curiosity, love, peace, courage and respect. These and other empowering values help us to make wise choices in our daily lives.

Through this P2B process, we will be nourishing our ethical intelligence, which as I stated earlier is our ability to ethically (using moral principles) self-regulate our thinking and behaviour. By so doing, we nurture our capacity for ethical leadership, which results in living an altruistic life. I find that adults need to discipline themselves (calendar/phone reminder) to take a daily P2B for 30 days so that it becomes a natural habit. You may experience, as many do, that your brain sends you strong messages that suggest that P2B is a waste of time, and you need to get on and do something useful! Don't worry, this is a natural reaction and will keep occurring until you train your brain to ignore this 'brain chatter'. When do I take a PAUSE to Be? Whenever I sense I need to stop, reflect and access my Self-energy to guide my thinking and behaviour. Sometimes I will P2B for a few minutes, but at other times it may only be a few seconds. Over time, being reflective before taking actions has become habitual and is particularly helpful in calming triggered emotions.

Teaching PAUSE to Be

Like Jane in the photo on the next page at Lake Wanaka in New Zealand, students are invited to remember the acronym PAUSE and what powers each letter represents and then

FIGURE 4.1 Teaching PAUSE to Be

commit time to practising PAUSE to Be daily. You can invite students to P2B during a lesson. We call this having a pause break, when you think your students will benefit from a mental re-set by being aware of the thoughts and feelings going on in their minds – you can call this the 'traffic' of their minds. You can signal that it's time to take a pause break by using a chime bar or other instrument. Pause breaks give us time to reset our internal system so that we can be fully present – to *be*.

Adults, please remember that it is vital for you to model the process too. The students will model themselves on your behaviour and will quickly pick up any inconsistencies between what you say and do. Your aim is to give students a tool that they will use in their lives, not just at school.

Last, in reading the following paragraphs, an important point for you to consider is to remember to adapt the language

I use to describe PAUSE to Be to suit the age and stage of your students. How I would express PAUSE to Be to 7-year-olds would be very different from adolescents or adults.

Now let's consider what the letters in PAUSE represent before teaching it to students

P is for Peace

You become peaceful when you connect with your innate peacefulness. This is achieved by being still and focusing on your breath, breathing slowly and more deeply. Because it is an active process, it appeals to all types of personality, but you will find some naturally take to it more quickly than others. Neuroscience tells us that, by breathing deeply, we calm the activity of our limbic system, the emotional centre of the brain. When PAUSE to Be is an established natural routine in the classroom, it is seen by all as an important daily practice. We have found that when the practice becomes a habit, it becomes a go-to when our internal worlds are feeling disturbed, wanting nourishment or when we want to consult the wisdom within us. Students will sometimes request time to P2B when they feel that they may become dysregulated.

A is for Attention

Now that you are peaceful and still, you can take your attention inward, to notice what is going on in your inner world. Many people find closing their eyes aids this process, whilst some prefer to keep their eyes open but to soften their gaze. You will become more aware of your feeling, sensations, thoughts and emotions. Don't judge them, but be curious about what they are telling you.

U is for Understanding

By pausing and taking your attention inward, you expand your understanding as to why your internal world is making you feel as you do. You may have parts of you that feel upset, frustrated, anxious, or happy and relaxed. All of them have a positive intention. Through this process of sensing how and what you are thinking and feeling, you gain clarity to understand about your inner world. This helps you to know which values you need to think about and experience to feel at peace. I sometimes think of dignity – the inherent worth that each of us possesses. A method which can be helpful is to introduce the idea of the Wisdom Star (see later in the chapter for details). Most students will be able to visualise a shining star, which radiates the values that they need to support themselves.

S is for Self-energy

As you PAUSE, slowing your breathing down, giving your attention to your inner world, you give space for your Self-energy to shine. Self-energy can be described as your heart-energy, as it is your source of your wonderful enhancing values, such as love, care and compassion. When you sense Self-energy is present, it is healing, calming the system down, helping you to feel at ease, able to be aware of what's going on inside and outside you in a loving non-judgemental way. When experienced, it helps you to feel confident, patient. I experience it as a 'warm glow' that helps me to *let go* and be truly me – allowing me to *be*. I have found this so useful just before I give a presentation to an unknown audience. You may experience Self-energy quite differently, as there's no right way!

E is for Ethical leadership

As you become aware of your self-energy, you are likely to feel more spacious inside. This means that you are inviting active parts of your personality to calm down, or you are inviting other parts to be constant in your thoughts. As a teacher, you may experience trying to give a lesson when a part of you is upset because of a personal message you have just received. Perhaps parts of you want your attention later, as they are trying to tell you something. For instance, a part may be upset because it feels hurt or shamed. Another part may be very excited about an event that may be happening, and yet another may feel sad. I have a part that is very excited as I am enjoying sharing PAUSE to Be with you in this chapter. The more you are aware of what makes up your inner world, the more you can lead your inner system more ethically.

Ethical leadership is the reward of the process, meaning that the choices and decisions you make in your life will be based on values/character traits that help you, us and our planet to flourish. Our world so needs ethical leaders at all levels in society.

How to teach a PAUSE to Be lesson

Teaching your students to PAUSE to Be – a specific active form of reflection/mindfulness – will help them to become naturally self-regulated, more resilient and able to maintain their own wellbeing. It gives them opportunities to reflect on values and behaviours that you may be highlighting in your classroom, which will help them nurture their ethical intelligence – their ability to ethically self-regulate their behaviour.

The following notes for your lessons will help you teach the students to PAUSE to Be. As I stated earlier, please adapt them for the age and stage of your students. You will need to give time to explaining in child-friendly ways what some of the terms mean. Start simply and build up understanding over a few weeks. I suggest you also create some visuals to help explain the distinct parts of the PAUSE to Be process.

I suggest that your students have daily PAUSE to Be sessions so that the process becomes a habit. Please remember that this means for you too! Remember, PAUSE times can be as short as a minute or an extended time. Invite the students to practise PAUSE at appropriate times in their day – at school and at home.

Link this teaching with giving the students an (age-appropriate) understanding of the main parts and functions of their brains, and how PAUSE strengthens the ability of their prefrontal cortex to regulate their responses to life; appropriately controlling their limbic system.

Example of a PAUSE to Be lesson

Ask primary-aged students to sit silently, relaxed but sitting upright (on their sit bones), hands in their laps. . . . If this is the first time sitting like this, you may need to explain how to sit comfortably and how to be aware of their breathing. Older students would normally be seated on their chairs. Deep breathing in for a count of five and out for a count of five has a calming effect on the mind.

You then say (please adapt the language to suit the age and stage of your students):

- "Do you ever think thoughts like these?"
- "Why did I do that?" "I wish I hadn't said that."

- "I feel rubbish and I can't help losing it."
- "I often feel very angry and then hurt someone."
- "I wish I could always feel happy."

Most people have similar thoughts and feelings, and wonder how they can be happier. People often think that they will be happier by distracting themselves by keeping busy, trying fresh activities or meeting new people. Sadly, this often doesn't help us to feel any happier, and we continue our search to feel good inside.

But! There is a way to help you keep your inner smile, that happy contented feeling that makes you like being you, helping you to get on better with other people. You may find the idea a bit weird or strange at first because it may be new to you. However, be patient because so many people have found that what I am going to tell you about has had wonderful effects on their lives. Would you like to find out more?

I think that the best way for you to understand what this is all about is to share an activity that I'm going to invite you to practise at least once a day. I think it will help you to remember the activity if I ask you to remember and think about a word: the word is PAUSE. Do you know what this word means? It means to stop doing something for a short time. I am using capital letters for PAUSE because each letter stands for something different that I am going to ask you to think about. When I have finished explaining what PAUSE means, I will then invite you to take a PAUSE and to share a few special moments with me.

The word PAUSE will remind you to make time in your busy day to stop, be still, close your eyes, and check out what you are thinking about and how you are feeling. This is called taking a PAUSE break. Taking daily PAUSE breaks gives you the chance to think about what you are thinking and feeling.

By doing this, you will be able to decide if what's going on inside you is helping you to enjoy your day or not.

Next you can decide which thoughts you would like to think about. If you choose happy thoughts, you will be amazed how good you will feel. Sometimes you may find this is difficult to do. If you do find it difficult to have happy thoughts, then be kind to yourself and perhaps have a chat with someone with whom you feel safe about how you are feeling. The more you practise PAUSE to Be, the more you will find it to be a very special way to help you to be happy.

You see, each letter in the word PAUSE reminds us of five life-enhancing, energy-giving powers that build your resilience, which is your ability to bounce back when you feel something has gone wrong. PAUSE will also help you to have a feeling of wellbeing, which is when you feel good about your life.

Explaining the word PAUSE

Let's look together at the letters of PAUSE and what energy powers they represent.

P stands for peace

I expect you know that when you feel peaceful you experience a deep feeling of being calm and safe. Now, when you need a top-up to feel peaceful, stop what you are doing and PAUSE. This means being still, closing your eyes and breathing deeply for at least ten slow breaths. By breathing deeply, you will find that you will slow down busy thoughts; you will gradually feel calm and peaceful, able to control your thinking and behaviour. This activity is called giving you a PAUSE break.

A stands for attention

You will know that people are sometimes asked to stand to attention, so that they can be still. Your teacher may say, "Please give me your attention," so she knows that you are listening. You can also think of attention as you being more aware about how you are thinking and feeling. By giving attention, you will know how your thoughts, feelings and emotions (strong feelings) are affecting your happiness. You may be feeling sad, angry, joyful, disgusted or fearful. Being aware of the emotions that you feel is the first step to helping you to be in control of them. During a PAUSE break you can check out what you are feeling and, if necessary, calm yourself down. Remember always to accept how you're feeling and, in whatever way you can, let the emotion know you are curious about it; that you want to know what has happened for this emotion to be present. If you can, send the feeling your love.

U stands for understanding

Being able to say, "Yes, I've got it! I understand why I'm feeling and thinking in this way." The more you learn about yourself and the world around you, the more your understanding of yourself and others will increase. Think that what you learn in school is a very special gift, as it gives you the knowledge and skills that will help you throughout your life. Grow your understanding a little bit every day, which will help you to make wise choices. In a PAUSE break, use the wisdom method of making wise decisions, allowing your inner wisdom to support your thinking: stop, breathe, think about the values that will help you and then take some action. This power helps you to make wise decisions and deepen your understanding of others.

You can decide which values will help you during the day and which skills you need to use, for example, patience, "I won't shout out."

S stands for self-energy

You are unique: there is no one who is exactly like you in the world. However, each of us may look and behave differently, but we all share something in common: we are all human beings, with our shared loving, healing, creative, curious, courageous, real self. Self-energy gives you the power of a helping energy that you feel when you PAUSE and allow your calm, compassionate, curious self to guide your thoughts. This healing power creates a feeling of wellbeing and happiness in us. When you take a PAUSE to Be, you will clear the space for you to be aware of the chatter going on in your mind and calm it down. You gain the power of self-leadership.

E stands for ethical leadership

This describes your ability to experiment and use your values to guide the ways you think and behave. This is the gift you develop when you PAUSE to Be. It helps you to make wise choices in life. When you take a PAUSE, you nurture your ethical intelligence – your ability to make wise choices. This helps you to take responsibility for your thoughts and behaviour for the good of yourself, others and the world. Taking a PAUSE allows you to connect to your values and to check that you are using them.

You will discover that the more you practise PAUSE, the more you will understand that it is your own personal energy power tool that will support your wellbeing each day of your life.

A PAUSE to Be activity for your students

At first you may want to read the following script. Please remember to pace your reading so that the students have time to understand the words. When you are more experienced with the PAUSE to Be routine, practise using your own language. This is an extended PAUSE to Be activity which uses the first and second special powers of PAUSE, peace and attention. Pausing to *be* helps us have access to the other three powers contained in the letters U, S and E, standing for understanding, self-energy and ethical leadership.

In a moment of silence, let us sit very still, close our eyes and feel relaxed. We can practise feeling peaceful by sitting comfortably, with straight backs, hands in our laps and with our eyes closed.

Now be aware of your breathing and silently concentrate on taking deeper breaths. As you breathe in slowly, count to five and do the same as you breathe out. With each breath, let your body become more and more relaxed. With each out breath, breathe out any thought or feeling that isn't helpful to you . . . with each in breath feel yourself breathing in quietness and calm . . .

Now let's use the power of our second letter, which is A. A, you remember, stands for attention, giving your attention to how you are feeling inside. In the next few moments as you are sitting calmly, give your attention to the thoughts you are having and how you are feeling today, without judging them or letting them overwhelm you.

Next let us use our imagination to help us to feel calm, full of peace. We are going to go on a walk to a special place in a beautiful wood.

Keeping your eyes closed, use your imagination to see yourself on a walk in a beautiful field. You have permission to be on this short walk, as you have been brought to it by some of your family. You are allowed to explore the field. You walk across it and see a shallow pond with ducks swimming on it. Beautiful butterflies are in the air. You walk by beautiful flowers and smell their energising scent. The sun is shining brightly and there are a few white clouds floating in the sky. As you walk across the field, you see a friend of yours coming towards you with a big grin. You feel happy and calm. Your friend is carrying a small box and says that in it is an amazing, coloured rock, which is a special gift for you. On it is written the name of the value that is your own special value. You are excited and, when the box is opened, you take your gift and read the name of the value written on it. "Yes! Thank you," you say to your friend. "This IS my favourite value." You then say cheerio to your friend and hurry back to your family to show them the gift you have been given.

Now slowly, and in your own time, return your attention to me . . .

You bring the PAUSE session to a conclusion with a general discussion.

Share with a partner what the value was that you were given. How did it make you feel, etc?

Another PAUSE to Be activity for your class – the Wisdom Star visualisation

Here is an example of a visualisation activity that I recommend, which students enjoy. You may like to have a picture of a star projected on a screen. In the early stages of learning about visualisation, some students may find it difficult to visualise, so it will help them to have a picture they can look at. Remember to adapt the words for the age and stage of your students.

Sitting comfortably and with dignity, close your eyes and give your attention to your breathing. . . . Focus on your breathing. . . . As you breathe out feel the sensation of your breath leaving your body.

If your mind wanders and thinks of other things, which is quite normal, then gently return the focus of your attention to your breath. As you become aware of your wandering mind and refocus on your breath, you are developing the skill of awareness.

For the next minute, focus on your breathing with an awareness of peacefulness . . . (In the early stages of practising this exercise, some find it helpful to focus if they say 'in' and 'out' in their minds as they breathe.)

. . . now visualise a beautiful, radiant shining star. . . . As you breathe deeply, your star appears to be brighter and full of energy. Now breathe normally and see your star's colours and its shape . . .

You can see that your shining star has lots of pulsating star-like points emerging from its core . . . what you are seeing is your values wisdom star . . . which contains many values, which are nourishing gifts to support you in your life. Your star is accessible to you whenever you need one of its gifts . . .

. . . now take a moment to sense what value would help you on your life's journey today . . . see the value pulsating calmly towards you on a beam of light, and the essence of you feeling its presence . . . merge yourself in this value, feeling its sublime qualities . . .

. . . which value did you chose? Name your value and sense by naming it for the powerful energy that it gives to you . . .

For the next few moments, take the time and space to experience your star's gift as energising sensations that will support you today and into the future . . .

Now gently, and in your own time, return your attention to the awareness of this room and the people within it.

Now give time for talking in pairs or groups before having a class discussion about the experiences the students had during this PAUSE to Be lesson.

I hope the Wisdom Star will provide lots of opportunities for discussion or journaling and enable your students to use values to help them self-regulate their behaviour.

For very young children, help them to focus on their breathing by introducing them to activities which will help them to relax and feel safe. You can place a cuddly toy on their tummies and invite them to breathe deeply but ensure their bodies are still, so that their toy remains on their tummies. Simple yoga exercises also help children to find their stillness.

Finally

From the feedback that I have received from teachers, I know that children can understand PAUSE to Be and enjoy using it, talking about it and making its practice a habit which supports their mental wellbeing and general health. Some teachers feel self-conscious and nervous about teaching P2B. If you are one of them, please take time to practise P2B with yourself so that you are familiar with it and gain in confidence before sharing it with students. Working together with other staff to trial activities also builds confidence.

Remember to give opportunities for the class to have short P2B breaks when you don't have a commentary but just give the students sufficient time to reset their internal worlds. You'll be amazed at how this will maintain a pro-social, positive atmosphere in your classroom. You'll be delighted too how this practice will help to enhance the quality of the students' work and their ability to self-regulate their behaviour.

I hope you are now inspired to teach PAUSE to Be to your students. Schools are sharing with me that P2B is used to great effect in assemblies, as well as during lesson time. In secondary education, it is being used by teachers across subject disciplines.

I think it's now time for you to take a simple, yet profound, P2B before we explore Chapter 5. Some people like to set a time prompt on their phone for a minute when they begin practising the basic P2B.

> *Sit quietly in a comfortable position, and focus your mind on breathing slowly and deliberately . . .*
>
> *If your mind wanders, gently bring it back to focus on your breathing . . .*

Making a regular routine in your day of what may seem a simple P2B will gradually enhance your consciousness, giving you many gifts, including clarity, a feeling of calm, enhanced energy and greater concentration. If you have the discipline to practise it for 30 days, you will find that it becomes a habit that will bring you life-enhancing gifts. Enjoy!

5

Ten insights into what underpins a conscious classroom

In this brief introductory chapter and the following ten chapters, I am very excited to introduce you to the insights I discovered from visiting the incredible conscious schools and their classrooms that have been on the roller-coaster journey of introducing Values-based Education (VbE).

These schools have felt confident to apply for the Values-based Education Quality Mark, which is an award of the charity the International Values-based Education Trust, known as the IVET Foundation. This honour is given to schools that demonstrate that they are embedding a deep awareness in children of the transformational role that values play in their lives. I believe that they are at the forefront of creating conscious classrooms, because young people demonstrate in their daily behaviour and character what I call *altruistic agency* – that inner drive to get up and do something for the good of others, which makes a positive difference – and really puts values behaviours into action.

 DOI: 10.4324/9781003681144-5

These inspirational schools are pioneering the principles of classroom consciousness. Their insights will give you practical examples that you can employ in whatever role you have in a school and/or in life generally. I think if you are a parent, you will be fascinated to learn about them and apply them in your home life.

I think it is important to emphasise that these selected schools are just a representative sample of so many wonderful schools that I am privileged to visit. I don't want to give you the impression that I have chosen an elite group that is unrepresentative of the majority of amazing VbE schools. I am also aware, and wish to acknowledge, that there are schools that are giving children amazing experiences and have been inspired by other values-based organisations other than VbE. It's important to mention the Global Alliance of Values-based Education (GAVE), which is drawing together organisations that are working towards the same end. I am honoured to be one of GAVE's founders.

I have chosen a variety of schools that are a representative sample of primary, secondary and special VbE schools. I am using data gathered when I made visits to assess them. Schools reapply for a Quality Mark, either the Standard or Enhanced, every four years. You can find details on the VbE website.

I am going to illustrate what I see as key aspects of conscious classrooms. The narrative sometimes includes the name of the school where I observed the aspect of consciousness in action at the time of my visit.

Studying the data seen in conscious classrooms and their schools, I have identified compelling evidence that shows that there are ten common features that indicate that students are being educated to ethically/morally self-regulate their thinking and behaviour, and achieve academically too. Such self-regulation, which can be described as enhanced consciousness or awareness, enables them to live more authentically, with greater congruity, with the benefit of a more harmonious inner world, giving them a heightened sense of wellbeing, resilience and ethical self-leadership. Importantly, it encourages students to develop a meaning and purpose for their lives, to have a moral compass, filling any existential vacuum by being actively pro-social citizens. Research also shows that it makes them better learners by encouraging academic diligence and relational trust (Lovat et al., 2009).

My ten insights into what underpins a conscious classroom

1. The leadership of the school is committed to the holistic development of VbE (Chapter 6).
2. A comprehensive ethical vocabulary, based on enhancing universal human values (Chapter 7).
3. Staff understanding that they are role models for VbE (Chapter 8).
4. Reflective practices creating an Inner Curriculum (Chapter 9).
5. Explicit and implicit teaching about values shown by all staff across the curriculum (Chapter 10).
6. A focus on mental wellbeing and health, emphasising care and compassion (Chapter 11).
7. A quality learning environment and empowering curriculum, that gives a sense of safety and dignity (Chapter 12).
8. Excellent staff relationships with each other, students and the community (Chapter 13).
9. Excellent behaviour and agency of students who live their values (Chapter 14).

10. Values-based Education being lived and celebrated in the school and community (Chapter 15).

I sense that you will enjoy reading about what's happening in schools that are nurturing conscious classrooms. So now we will explore these transformational insights in the following Chapters 6–15.

6

The leadership of the school is committed to the holistic development of VbE

I describe conscious leaders in this way:

> Leaders are seen as Self-aware and Self-led, open to their own process, possessing a comprehensive range of humane qualities; empowering them with the will to embrace challenge and complexity; helping them and their organisation to flourish.

In May 2023, I was honoured to speak at the United Nations in Geneva about why we need ethical leadership which is values based if we are to achieve the UN's Sustainable Development Goals. I argued that the development of ethical leadership begins in schools, initially with adults and then with children. I am very proud of the leaders of VbE schools, as they recognise the importance of conscious leadership.

DOI: 10.4324/9781003681144-6

A key feature of outstanding, conscious, values-based leadership is that, despite the pressures that society places on schools, the senior leadership of the school remains upbeat and positive and has a clear vision (consciousness) based on their values about the direction of travel for their school.

Leaders are aware that the conscious school and its classrooms must focus on altruistic agency by extending *natural altruism*, which is innate and instinctive, such as care for a child, to what is known as *extended altruism*. This is not naturally spontaneous but needs to be cultivated in conscious homes and schools by making altruistic behaviour habitual. An example would be showing respect to all by opening a door for another person, irrespective of age, gender or any other factor. The staff of the school would model this habit to the students. I'm sure you can think of other examples. By building extended altruism in the school, it then extends outwards to create a society based on *cultural altruism*. With the expediential growth and influence of AI, I predict that there will need to be a huge shift towards enabling students to develop the full range of human intelligences that will strengthen their character, as illustrated in this book.

Can you imagine a future society with cultural altruism at its core? I have witnessed such altruistic behaviours in Scandinavian countries, such as Iceland and Sweden, which seem to achieve a greater balance between individual rights and collective responsibilities. My visits to many countries have made me realise that the 'true' values of a country are transmitted in what I describe as its *hidden culture*: not the culture that is projected or talked about in the media, but the way people feel towards each other and in their relationships.

What would you say are the 'true' values of your country? Are you beginning to see why there is a need for conscious classrooms, which will help transform the current culture, which I would argue is self-serving?

Conscious leaders are proud of their schools, as the sign at Ledbury Primary School shows, and declare to their communities that they are outward-facing values-based schools.

They are reflective, don't take things personally, understand themselves and display a high level of Self-leadership. They handle complexity deftly and have their focus on their own school's mission and values rather than trying constantly to please a perceived external agenda, which in my view is nearly impossible to deliver and often the cause of so much mental illness in the profession. They are leaders who are skilled in relationship-building, promoting collaboration and fostering good ideas with their enthusiasm. Such leaders encourage authentic, open, honest communication, which builds trust and harmony. They can release the creative dynamic of each member of staff through their open manner and encouragement of sharing ideas. They have deep respect for others and have defined the

FIGURE 6.1 Ledbury Primary School, welcome sign, highlighting that the school is values-based.

school's values-based ethos to ensure that it creates a culture where there is never a hierarchy of relationships, only of roles. Conscious leaders are also determinedly realistic, only taking on what the school has the capacity to deliver.

In the photo are the head, Peter Dunmall, and some of the large staff team at Fielding Primary School in Ealing on a staff training day. Through his words and actions, Pete is prepared to be a role model and totally committed to VbE in the school.

Another head, Natalie Hackett, at New Lubbesthorpe School in Leicestershire, described to me how and why she decided to lead the school to be a part of VbE. She spoke with so much enthusiasm and commitment:

> We are so proud of our school. We grew it from new in 2019 and the first thing we did was our values-based curriculum.

FIGURE 6.2 Headteacher and staff being enthusiastic role models for VbE at Fielding School, Ealing, London.

> From lots of research and working alongside other Owls Trust schools, we chose core values, which made sense to the children. We knew that, as the school grew, we would have an excellent community. VbE is about everything in our school. It allows our children to understand what a value is and how it can guide their behaviour and thinking – everything they need in life.

At the same school, I spoke with Phoebe, the values lead. Her enthusiasm and commitment to the school being values based embraced everything she told me about her leadership role. When I asked her about the impact of VbE on the children, she answered:

> It helps children to value their behaviour, leading to better attainment. By their having values, they are kind, and they are listening and showing respect. By their doing that, they are making appropriate choices – they are not falling out and therefore not affecting learning time. They are listening, focusing; we are seeing the results in our attainment data because they are retaining information, having clearer mindsets and they are focusing more positively.

I expect you noticed that Phoebe referred to the children as having clearer mindsets, which is what a conscious classroom enables the students to have. Incidentally, the CEO of the Owls Trust, of which this school is a part, said to me that:

> The Trust wanted all their schools to be VbE schools because they felt that if behaviour and attitudes are right then other things such as standards will naturally follow.

Another great conscious school community can be found at Messingham Primary School, near Scunthorpe, North Lincolnshire. Bethany Rose, the values lead, speaks so poignantly about Values-based Leadership at the school being compassionate:

> Values-based leadership at our school is compassionate leadership. Everybody in the school is involved in their different roles with leading and promoting a values-based approach. It is therefore evident in all areas of the school community. Adults are strong role models and encourage pupils to take on responsibility for themselves and others. Leaders empower and encourage others to develop their own potential. The school actively supports families. Compassionate values-based leadership informs all of the school's actions, provision and decision-making; at times it is demanding – requiring a courageous and principled stance – but will always reap benefits for the individuals and the school as a whole.

Beth goes on to say:

> The quality of leadership is paramount, because without it a values-based school does not develop. The headteacher/principal is key because he/she is the principal architect of the school's vision. We observe that having the capacity to dream (use creative imagination) brings transformational positive energy (inspiration) into the formation of a VbE school – a prime characteristic of an altruistic leader. This, coupled with the seemingly endless capacity to access their own reservoir of uncontaminated self-energy, enables the leader(s) to remain stable and focused in an educational context of incomparable complexity and challenge. It

> is through their commitment, drive, care and ability to inspire others that the leader creates a sustainable school culture based on VbE, which has the active support of all members of staff, ensuring consistency of practice across all aspects of school life. Others will play a major part in the leadership of the school. However, I would argue that a VbE school encourages all members of the school, both adult and children, to be seen as leaders, taking personal responsibility for their thoughts and behaviour and sustaining an ethical vocabulary.

I sometimes take part in a team of trainers, with my focus on ethical leadership, for my friend Floyd Woodrow and his transformational Compass for Life Movement. Floyd has supported Warren Farm School in Birmingham, which helps children to understand the skills which Floyd's Compass model promotes. Having a Super North Star is key – a meaning and purpose which drives behaviour. The school has also embraced VbE to create a curriculum and school ethos that is purpose-driven and rooted in values.

The headteacher, Simon Taylor, is a leader with a clear vision of future education, who wants all that they are doing at Warren Farm School to help change the face of education. He said to me:

> My Super North Star is a school that changes the face of education. One of the ways I want to do that is through implementing the importance of values in education for the children, the community and parents as well.

The character education lead at the school, Andrew Davis, elaborated further:

> Values-based Education resonates deeply with our work at Warren Farm. Neil and Jane Hawkes articulate why values matter so powerfully, and that alignment has driven us to be equally intentional about how we develop character through a structured, lived curriculum, with purposeful space for reflection.

When Jane and I met with some of the students at Warren Farm School, we were met with the strapline on a display board: "It's who we are, not what we do," which is the foundation for values-based character development.

Conscious leader practices

To complete this leadership section, I would like to share with you some practices for you to consider which will foster conscious compassionate leadership.

- The headteacher/principal communicates their values and related behaviours clearly to members of staff, e.g. "One of my values is integrity, so being honest is central to my behaviour." By so doing, they create a moral culture based on universal, human values such as dignity, trust and compassion.
- The leadership is clear that staff personal values must be in alignment with the school's stated values, which ensures that trust and harmony are central to the school's ethos and that the school doesn't suffer from a 'split personality'. For instance, if respect is a school value, then members of staff will not shout inappropriately at students, be sarcastic or shaming.

- Leaders are clear about their expectations, making it clear what constitutes their 'bottom line', e.g. zero tolerance of dishonesty. They act decisively after taking all factors into account. Such behaviour creates a feeling of safety and cohesion in the staff, no one having to second-guess what the leader will tolerate in the organisation.
- Leaders lead by example, are Self-aware and ethically Self-led. They have an understanding about their inner world of thoughts, feelings and emotions and the potential effects they have on others. They embody self-efficacy and are resilient, optimistic and create a sense of hope for the future. They understand that, at their core, they can access wisdom.
- Leaders care and value themselves, and treat others with respect and with equity – there are no favourites!
- Leaders are real and confident to acknowledge their own fallibility and common humanity.
- Leaders are empathic listeners, being able to be reflective and give appropriate, not necessarily instant, advice and leadership.
- Leaders think carefully about the school's routines, structures and practices to ensure that they are values based. Examples include thinking carefully about unintentional consequences of school practices such as staff emails, avoiding being 'email warriors', putting unreasonable pressure on staff in the evenings and weekends to respond to an email request. Ensuring that shaming children through practices such as putting children's names on 'the dark cloud' in the classroom are not introduced, and positive 'values charters' are used instead to highlight and model appropriate agreed-upon classroom behaviour. They realise that the more the children live the school's values, the less there is a need for rules to control behaviour.

- Teachers see themselves as leaders of their conscious classrooms.
- Support staff also see themselves as leaders and role models who support the ethos and workings of the conscious classroom.
- Throughout the school, leaders will promote open, honest, caring and compassionate relationships. They see mistakes as opportunities for growth, thereby creating an experimental and experiential focus for learning. Taking appropriate chances and using initiative is valued in the school as a way of promoting open growth mindsets that embrace challenge and critical and ethical thinking. They generally have an open-door policy and are approachable to all staff.
- Governors or trust members are supportive in all areas of school life and attend school events. They are very visible to the children and are regular visitors to the school, so children and staff have a positive relationship with them.
- Children too are also seen as leaders, working alongside teachers to develop agency through responsibility. At Messingham Primary School, they have values ambassadors, who arrange charity donations for the homeless, fundraising for Comic Relief and selling poppies in the lead up to Remembrance Day. Wildlife ambassadors meet with the headteacher to improve the wildlife at the school. Student leaders also are front of house for parents' evenings. A key part of their role is to support younger children and be the link between them and the school's leadership team.

These real examples can be generalised about the quality of leadership across the VbE family of schools. Importantly, I want to stress that because VbE is about the creation of a whole school culture, the conscious school and its classrooms, it can only be successful if the leadership team is fully committed to its implementation and success. Otherwise, it becomes what I have termed a school with laminated values – the values are displayed on the walls but not in the hearts and lives of the people.

Reflect on your leadership

- In whatever role(s) you have, how would you describe your leadership?
- Based on the examples in this chapter, are there aspects of leadership that you would like to adopt into your own thinking and behaviour as a leader?
- By considering the list above of conscious leader practices, what actions could you take to be a more conscious leader?

I hope this reflection has helped you to consider your own thinking and behaviour as a leader, whatever role you play in the organisation or in other aspects of your life. I trust that you now feel empowered to enhance your own leadership behaviour by reflecting on this chapter's insights. Please remember that whatever role you play in life, you are a leader!

7

A comprehensive ethical vocabulary based on enhancing universal human values

Once the leadership team and staff are all on the 'values bus', as the headteacher of a secondary school in Eastbourne remarked to me, then the creation of a comprehensive ethical vocabulary, based on values, is the next stage. I described the process for this in Chapter 3 – The Guide to creating a Conscious School and Classrooms.

Bridget Knight, on the next page, is the CEO for Values-based Education and was the Head of Eardisley CE Primary School in Herefordshire. Bridget epitomises the qualities of leadership described in the previous section. Her values display in the photo reflects her belief that our values give us the roots and wings for our lives. She actively nurtured students' values consciousness by encouraging them to be courageous advocates for values. They developed their critical awareness, looking to be curious about and

DOI: 10.4324/9781003681144-7

FIGURE 7.1 Creating a conscious school and classrooms

sometimes to challenge what they saw as the limiting values of the adult world, such as selfishness, greed and intolerance.

They are regularly invited to take part in Pupils2Parliament and formally debate real bills that are making their way through Parliament. Their recommendations are recorded in Hansard. Bridget insightfully told me that:

> When pupils of ten and eleven lend their moral muscle in this far-reaching way, it brings hope for the trajectory of their own lives, and for our country.

It is important to keep the values vocabulary relevant and current. At Worplesdon Primary School in Surrey, the school's ethical vocabulary is reviewed yearly to ensure that its twenty-two values are the appropriate values on which the school should focus. They told me that, because of the values vocabulary, their students were becoming much more articulate and could talk about the values they and others were demonstrating (values consciousness). Furthermore, during conflict resolution, children could show their developing ethical intelligence by talking about the value that was not guiding their behaviour! Classroom displays highlight values language, and school planning demonstrates how the values language is included in teaching time.

School inspectors sometimes remark about a school's values. In the Ofsted Report for Chantry Primary Academy (June, 2023), they wrote:

> Chantry Primary Academy is a school where pupils are happily 'learning for life'. The school's values of aspiration, respect, unity, integrity, independence, enjoyment and quality are practised in the daily lives of the pupils.

Chantry is a part of the Pioneer Learning Trust, a values-based trust based in Luton. Its CEO, Cori Bateman, has been one of the outstanding pioneers of VbE, and her influence as a VbE adviser has spread to numerous schools.

Some schools, such as Madley Primary School in Herefordshire, develop an exceptional experiential, creative curriculum through which the values vocabulary flows. Outdoor learning is an integral part of the teaching and learning at Madley, cultivating a respect and appreciation for our natural world, whether through activities on site in the school grounds, at their dedicated forest school site or on one of the many curriculum visits undertaken by each class. Values are explained explicitly during assemblies, class assemblies and within the PSHE programme of study and implicitly through the way lessons and activities are planned. Co-operative tasks, for example, are embedded within their Dimensions themes, whilst challenging tasks that require critical thinking allow students to build resilience and develop greater communication skills. The school was honoured by a visit from Prince William and Catherine, Princess of Wales. They were enthralled to observe and interact with students at Forest School, which is part of the Duchy of Cornwall's Estate, seeing an outstanding example of values in action, such as trust, responsibility and agency.

A mantra that VbE promotes, to help students understand what defines a value is, "A value is a principle that guides our thinking and behaviour." Children never fail to enthral me by their originality, depth of thinking and sense of the spiritual, which I define as the non-materialist inner world of thoughts, feelings and emotions. An example of this insight – the ability to sense the internal world – occurred when I asked a Year 6 student at Madley what a value is. She thoughtfully replied:

> A value basically is an inanimate object; you can hold and see, but only if you show it correctly. So, if you have a value and look at it, it will be like a wisp of colour that will encircle you. And if you find someone else not quite showing a value, you can always halve that spirit and then they will have it too. If you and that person share the spirit equally with everyone in the world, then everyone will be happy and have their own values such as compassion.

Listening to these words was a real wow moment for me. How did you react to her words and why?

An activity that I find helps children to think deeply about their own values and the role they play in their lives is to ask them to draw their core values as well as naming them. I remember a student drawing a colourful picture of him being tolerant by showing him with his family when they were obviously all shouting at each other!

Encouraging families to think about the values that guide them as a family is also another great exercise that helps parents to see the importance of the values vocabulary in their homes.

At another school, Broughton Fields Primary School, a long-standing VbE school in Milton Keynes, the heart of the curriculum is the values vocabulary. I saw this in all the lessons I observed – so many special loving moments, as shown when children say to whom they are grateful. "Thank you for looking after me," said a student to her teacher.

Values words are used explicitly in lessons and implicitly during all aspects of the curriculum. Students can readily identify the values that they are using, and staff constantly reinforce the language of values. In a high-energy, engaging Year 3 lesson, students identified values that they need to achieve. These included aspiration, determination, resilience and responsibility. I loved the 'words wave' – new to me – which gave all a chance to voice values that they think are important by holding up their values written on whiteboards.

At VbE schools, I am so often aware, as I was at Broughton Fields, that they have thought deeply about how they introduce the values vocabulary to children with special needs (SEND). At Broughton Fields, I was moved by the calm and purposeful inclusive atmosphere which promoted the understanding of values. There is no doubt that the care, respect and love that all children are shown are central to this process.

At Ben Rhydding Primary School in Ilkley, West Yorkshire, classrooms are also inclusive environments, evidenced by the use of Zones of Regulation, which the head, Peter Simms, says develops ethical intelligence by giving a common language to navigate emotions. For older pupils, this includes Habits of Mind, developed by Arthur L. Costa and Bena Killick in their book *Learning and Leading with Habits of Mind* (ASCD,

2008), which encourages pupils to reflect on key learning dispositions in more depth. This inclusivity is built up in layers, with whole school approaches such as Philosophy for Children (P4C), which creates communities of critical thinkers and initiatives, like Values Ambassadors in Year 6 who promote values in school. The school is also inclusive of SEND children with low sensory levels, creating autistic-sensitive environments for them, as shown in the use of widgets and visual timetables to support communication and learning, and by adding visual symbols to text, making it more accessible and understandable.

Examples of highly conscious therapeutic schools for children with special needs deserve a big 'shout out', such as Wilds Lodge School, Rutland, where I was a regular visitor during the leadership of the inspirational Robin Lee, who, in my view, created the gold standard in SEND provision prior to his untimely death.

Under Robin as owner and leader, this independent therapeutic special school invested in the children rather than its owners and shareholders. Consequently, the students, aged between 7 and 18 years of age, benefitted from an outstanding environment with the very best of furnishings, curriculum provision, structures and routines. Above all, excellent interpersonal relationships were central to Robin's educational philosophy, which enabled students to feel safe and secure and become the best version of themselves that they could be. I remember him telling me that the kitchen and dining room should be at the centre of the school, because food was the constant for the students around which the school's life revolved. The meals were delicious, and the aroma from the kitchen created a feeling of homeliness. Family service of the meals ensured that students were involved in the process, and there were great conversations, often using the values vocabulary, between staff and students. Sadly, some schools look on mealtimes as something they must provide but are far from being pleasant events, far from being an extension of effective relational learning.

Robin was very dismissive of private schools that did not give the best to students because of their materialistic focus on profit-making. I will remember him for being the embodiment of Maya Angelou's words, "People will never forget how you made them feel." Because of Robin's deep sense of commitment to young people with special needs, the school received the Enhanced Values Quality Mark – an outstanding highly conscious school and classrooms.

Also, I want to mention two other special schools that are outstanding as conscious schools, which put emphasis on enabling young people to use and act on an ethical vocabulary. These are Silverwood School in Wiltshire and Tudor Lodge Therapeutic School, a relatively new school in Lincolnshire, both of which are showing how profoundly VbE creates the culture that fosters conscious classrooms.

Emma Rossiter, the inspirational values lead at Silverwood School, says that the quality of relationships and learners' sense of trust and belonging are unconditionally important in all interactions. She reminds us to look at behaviour as the communication of unmet needs rather than something to be punished. That to enable young people to be their best selves, we need to place relationships, belonging and trust at the heart of everything – not something that is conditional. Such a shift benefits everyone and especially our most vulnerable learners, be that because of poverty, neurodiversity, childhood trauma or all of these. This is especially important when pupils are struggling with emotional regulation and behaviour skills.

Silverwood School have aligned their VbE with work described by Anthony Benedict and Alan Braven in the book

Educating Everyone: An Introduction to Relational Inclusion (Taylor & Francis, 2025). The 5 Principles of Relational Inclusion dovetail with VbE's Conscious Classroom and Silverwood School's core values. This enables adults and learners to be always guided and supported in a relationally safe way, and challenging behaviour is always viewed as the communication of unmet needs.

Silverwood Value	*Relational Inclusion Principles*
Co-operation	Everything is based on relationships, relationships, relationships.
Courage	We accept all emotions, but not all behaviours.
Honesty	We identify and address the cause of behaviour. Difficulties, not the systems.
Perseverance	We believe that if a child could do better, then they would.
Respect	We create a culture of compassion and repair.
Kindness	All these principles in action together.

Deborah Seragusa, the head of Tudor Lodge Therapeutic School, told me:

> Our school is a home-from-home environment, built on strong values that underpin everything we do. We believe that children want to succeed, even when they do not yet have the skills to do so. By celebrating positives – no matter how big or small – we build confidence and a strong sense of self-worth, creating a secure foundation for growth. Guided by our values, we provide a safe, supportive environment, where every child feels valued, develops a sense of belonging and is empowered to achieve their full potential.

Last in this section, I would like to highlight the amazing work that I see in the Early Years Foundation Stage. I owe so much in my own understanding of quality education to colleagues who work with the youngest children.

Jane and I recently visited Chantry Primary Academy and Southfield Primary Academy Foundation stages, as they had been audited for the Early Years Values Quality Mark. I had been asked to present the awards at their school assemblies. Later we had our photo taken with some of the children and the values lead at Chantry. I came away thrilled to see such quality education in these two schools, which are a part of the Pioneer Learning Trust in Luton.

I asked the early years values lead at Chantry why children aged 2, 3 and 4 need to learn about values and what they gained from them. She replied:

> We think it's important for our youngest children to learn about values so that they are included in the whole school values approach that we take.
>
> We also know that the three prime areas of the early years foundation stage: communication and language; personal, social and emotional development; fine and gross motor skills development can all be woven in through values.
>
> We know that once those prime areas in the foundation stage are established, children feel safe at school. They are happy, they have good connections with adults and their friends. All the academic progress comes as soon as those three prime areas are solid.
>
> So, we weave all our values into our three prime areas to make sure all our children feel included and happy and safe at school.
>
> We have amazing role models here at Chantry from our teachers and support staff, who know that, once values are embedded, children thrive.

I hope that the examples I have shared help you to understand the profound changes in consciousness that happen in schools when students are given access to an ethical vocabulary based on values. I have always argued that maths and science have their distinct vocabularies, so why not ethics!

For you to ponder

- Do you have some personal core values that drive your thinking and behaviour?
- To what extent do you use a values-based vocabulary in your daily life?
- Do others know what your values are? Ask a friend what they think your values are.
- Are values made explicit in your home life? How?

8

Staff understand that they are role models for VbE

I'm hoping that you are being inspired by reading about actual classrooms that are filled with enhanced consciousness.

I'm now going to put the focus on a very important insight, one that's easy to say but for all of us challenging to be, especially if we are upset, tired or distracted. It is being a role model that students can emulate as someone who lives their values.

I sometimes ask people on training days to put up their hands if they are perfect. Once in Brisbane, Australia, a man put up his hand, and I asked him why he thought he was perfect. He simply answered, "Because my Mum says I am!" Everyone burst out laughing, as he did.

The truth, of course, is that none of us is perfect. This is an important point to remember when we aim to be a role model for VbE. We need compassion when we get it wrong. For instance, on one of those days when we feel overwhelmed and behave in an irritated way or make a remark that is inappropriate, we need

DOI: 10.4324/9781003681144-8

FIGURE 8.1 "We are the founders of our own story"

to be super conscious and make repair as quickly as possible. Students will admire you more if you are prepared to apologise and show your authenticity. Remember that life is a journey and our aim is to be the best version of ourselves that we can be.

Such a person is Beth Rose, the Values Lead at Messingham Primary School. Here she is standing in front of an impactful display with the words, "We aspire to be our best selves. We are the founders of our own story."

I asked Beth how conscious she is about being a good role model for others. Here's her reply:

> I am deeply conscious of the responsibility I carry as a role model and the privilege it is to shape not only minds, but hearts. While I can teach short division, the craft of a relative clause or explain how the choices of the Vikings still echo today, I believe the greatest impact I have as a

> teacher lies in the values and behaviours I model each day. As children leave primary school and step into the next chapter of their lives, the maths methods will change, the grammar rules will evolve and the history they study will shift. What remains constant are their core values, how they treat others, how they view the world, the belief they carry that they really do matter and that their actions can make a monumental difference. Because of this, in all that I do, I strive to model kindness, respect and integrity, ensuring every child feels seen, valued and empowered to carry these values, not just in school, but at home, in the wider community and through every step along their journey of life. Collectively, alongside children, staff, parents and governors, we adapted our school motto to, 'We aspire to be the best versions of ourselves; we are the founders of our own story'. This deeply resonates with me and underpins all that I do. I model to the children that we are ever-evolving and ever-growing, continually reflecting on our story so far and thoughtfully considering how we choose to shape the chapters that come next.

Beth's final reflections come from two voices she holds closest to her heart – her daughters, Belle and Florence. Their opinions matter to her beyond measure. For them, she will continue to strive to be the very best version of herself, knowing that the moral compass and core values they absorb today will guide them as they grow, thrive and pursue all that they dare to dream of. For Beth, to play even a small part in shaping the people they become is both her greatest responsibility and her greatest privilege.

> My mum is an incredible and super talented woman who is always there for you whenever you need her. No matter

> what, she is always an inspiration to the people around her and shows each and every value every single day, even if things are tough.
>
> 10-year-old Belle

> Mummy is my role model because she makes me feel brave.
>
> 4-year-old Florence

To be viewed through the eyes of children is both humbling and inspiring, a reminder that the greatest impact we have is often felt, not taught. To be seen as someone who inspires bravery, kindness and strength is an absolute honour and a powerful reminder that role modelling is found not in grand gestures, but in the quiet consistency of how we live our values each day.

Some years ago, I audited a school in Lincoln with the unusual name of St. Peter at Gowts Primary CE School. I had got to know it well following a whole staff training in VbE. The headteacher at that time was Charlotte Hickerton, who not only embraced VbE but embodied it as a conscious leader. I wrote in the school's audit report:

> Outstanding! Outstanding! Outstanding! I cannot praise enough the positive attitude of the staff and how *they act as excellent role models for the children*. The Head and Senior Leadership team are an exceptionally positive team, and their infectious enthusiasm pervades the whole school, creating outstanding relationships that the pupils emulate.

In acting as good role models, all staff spoke about students positively. They established warm relationships and aimed to be firm, fair and kind in every situation. This was supported by senior leaders modelling a 'no shouting or intimidation' approach, using effective behaviour management strategies like restorative justice.

Since becoming head, Charlotte had raised morale by showing staff that they really matter as people. She had ensured that everyone had access to quality continuous professional development (CPD). This had led to staff feeling more confident and relaxed, which I think is a key to being able to be a good role model.

At another conscious school, Stepping Stones Short Stay School – a special school in Lancaster – I recorded in their audit report that members of staff were outstanding ambassadors and role models for Values-based Education. They helped students to understand that they had to be role models too.

When talking about being a role model to staff in schools, I often draw their attention to their ability to have shining eyes. It has been my experience that adults with shining eyes have a positive, can-do approach to life. They are confident in their relationships with students, and they leave their troubles away from school.

At Pear Tree School, an outstanding residential special school on a farm near Darlington, members of staff are outstanding role models for Values-based Education. All appear to have 'shining eyes' – even the horses, which students care for as part of their curriculum. Inspirational headteacher David Bartlett, MBE, epitomises what I wrote in the previous chapter about conscious leadership.

In my audit report of the school, I wrote:

> The development of respectful relationships is central to the school's success in both helping the pupils recover from their traumas and being educated. Members of staff have received high-quality training so that they are aware of the best ways to follow a step-by-step approach to helping children

> to self-regulate their internal worlds. They skilfully avoid positively reinforcing negative behaviour, new pupils soon realising that they will not be rewarded for inappropriate behaviour. The school employs high quality members of staff who have the capacity to educate a group of vulnerable children by being excellent values role models.
>
> For instance, I observed a riding lesson in the arena, which showed how staff support students working with horses. They enabled students to develop courage, integrity, respect, responsibility and kindness to a very high level. Learning to ride and taking care of a horse helps pupils to develop mindfulness: moment-to-moment, non-judgemental attention, which has a profound effect on the healthy development of the internal world of the student.

Being a role model requires a great deal of introspection, which I found as headteacher of West Kidlington School. The staff often said to me that being in a values-based school had had a profound effect on them as people. Teaching and reflecting about values, and then modelling them positively, changed their thinking and behaviour.

Over to you . . .

- Who has been a role model for you?
- How conscious are you about being a good role model for others?
- Are you aware what sort of role model you are? If you are comfortable, ask some others for their insights about you.
- How do you help others to be good role models?

9

Reflective practices creating an inner curriculum

I hope that after thinking about being a role model in the last chapter, you will find this one inspires you to instil reflective practice as the key method to heighten consciousness. There is no doubt in my mind that reflective practices have enhanced my life both personally and professionally. May I remind you that I wrote a longer chapter on this subject in Chapter 4.

I am delighted that so many schools are actively thinking about how they can give their students the gift of being calm. This quality has been one of the casualties of our modern over-stimulated world, where children seem rarely to be given the opportunity to experience a feeling of peacefulness, calm and even boredom. I think that reflection is vitally important for mental wellbeing and should be considered the fourth R in Education. I was pleased to read that Dan Siegel the inter-personal neuroscientist thinks so too! He said, "Reflection transforms the brain by developing the neural connections in

DOI: 10.4324/9781003681144-9

the prefrontal cortex." Is this why meditators have been found to have a thicker prefrontal cortex in their brains?

As a headteacher, I was convinced that having time for reflection was one of the main reasons that the quality of education improved in the school. Students learned how to be still, calm yet fully aware, which led to them being able to integrate their learning experiences so that they became more effective learners.

In Chapter 4 I introduced you to PAUSE to Be (P2B). Worplesdon Primary School in Surrey has given a lot of staff training time to thinking about how to help students have access to an inner curriculum through P2B. The headteacher led its introduction in assemblies, and this has now been successfully adopted across all classrooms in the school. Staff and children report that they enjoy being given more opportunities to stop and reflect on their thoughts and feelings. Staff have also created classroom calm corners, and worry boxes where children can post their concerns. Students use PAUSE bottles which gives them the opportunity, as the contents settle, to calm themselves down. Teachers create more opportunities for time to think. They use Russian dolls for children to understand their own layers of personality and use chime bars to gain children's attention for P2B breaks. Above all, the staff model being calm and reflective, consciously giving time to deeply listen to children. All this creates a learning culture where effective learning can take place, where both adults and students are more relaxed and connected.

In a Swindon school, part of the White Horse Trust, I witnessed staff creating calm times at the beginning of the day, with the children sitting in a circle with a candle flame burning in the centre. Circle times create wonderful opportunities for silent reflection.

Simon Poote, the early years lead at Long Crendon School in Buckinghamshire, creates a meaningful reflection time after lunch. The reception children know to come in and sit on the carpet, showing that they are ready by holding a hand on their chests with a thumb up. After all the children are still and focused, he leads them in a reflective visualisation, which is usually very creative and engaging.

If you want ideas, I recommend you look at the fabulous creations of Marneta Viegas, founder of Relax Kids (relaxkids.com). To support children's wellbeing, Relax Kids advisers are pleased to give staff training.

If you are a parent or Early Years teacher, then take a look at Conscious Stories by Andrew Newman (consciousstories.com) for a series of bedtime stories purpose-built to support parent-child connection in the last 20 minutes of the day.

Giving staff time to think about how they can calm children down and the training and resources they need is very important if you want to ensure that staff will feel comfortable engaging in reflective practices. Introducing reflective practices without time to explore the range of supportive ideas can lead to staff feeling unsure and hesitant. Pixies Hill Primary School in Hemel Hampstead devoted a whole day for psychotherapist Jane to give each class a demonstration lesson so that staff could be more familiar with breathing and reflective techniques. Staff are now more confident, which ensures continuity of practice throughout the school.

Under the leadership of its first headteacher, Hannah Wilson, Aureus School, a secondary school in Didcot, Oxfordshire, introduced mindfulness activities at the beginning of each day, ranging from mindfulness art to mindful movement.

On the other side of the world in Brisbane, Australia, inspirational teacher Dr Michael Downey successfully introduced reflective practices in several secondary schools. His testimony speaks volumes about values and reflective practices, and is a fitting conclusion for this section:

> My friend, author Parker J Palmer, taught me that teaching is a three-way relationship between teacher, students and subject matter. Like other important relationships, this relationship needs attention. It needs to be nourished and nurtured.
>
> Unfortunately, the chaos and constant overload that is 'normal' in most schools and classrooms leave little, if any, opportunity for reflective practices. In this context, it can be quite radical and subversive to take a moment to stop, slow down and calm the overactive, often exhausted, mind. I found taking 5–7 minutes at the start of each lesson allowed my students and myself to all 'be' in the room together. It encouraged us to respect what we were doing together. My students knew and understood that I valued 'them'. We learned to value our co-operation. Regardless of what we say we value, I learnt that 'reflective practices' are nothing unless we 'practise reflection' as a priority.
>
> Like it or not, our actions, our practices, are what articulate our values most convincingly.

Your chance to reflect

If you have a mobile phone with a timer, set it to ring in 3 minutes.

> During that time, just soften your gaze, relax, and breathe a little more deeply.

> Focus your mind on your in and out breath. If your mind wanders, gently bring it back to your breath.

This simple yet profound exercise is an excellent habit that, if practised at least daily for 30 days, will be ingrained in your routines. You will find that over time it will increase your ability to be still and able to focus your concentration, making you more aware, conscious of all that happens in your life. You will be living more in the present!

- How can you help others to find the life-enhancing properties of reflection?

10

Explicit and implicit teaching about values shown by all staff across the curriculum

The previous chapter gave you some insights into reflective practices, so you may like to bring the insights to this chapter by perhaps pausing to *be*, if you sense it would be helpful to have a mindful break as you read this and other chapters.

In this chapter, we will look at some of the ways that schools are teaching about values, both explicitly when teaching about them and implicitly in the language that teachers use, and in the general curriculum and life of the school.

In VbE schools, values are often an integral and explicit part of assemblies, as well as during values lessons and the curriculum in general. Assemblies bring together staff and students in a shared experience to learn about values through stories and by reflecting on the lives of people who have lived their values.

 DOI: 10.4324/9781003681144-10

At Little Hill Primary School in Leicester, a part of the Owls Trust, the school gives a focus on one of the school's values for a month, giving an introduction with definition and examples and a reference to a book that highlights the value, followed by famous people who have shown the value. Importantly, the school takes the students deeper into thinking about the value by giving scenarios with real-life applications and the impact of the value for life at the school. The headteacher demonstrated his leadership of VbE, recognising that VbE is an educational journey. At assembly, he displayed his many talents as a teacher. His relational skills and careful structuring of assembly gave the students an understanding of the value of the month.

I have always loved taking assemblies and watching others who inspire children to be the best versions of themselves that they can be. Over the years, I have observed that there are several elements that make a VbE assembly of quality. These are:

- Ensuring that there is a sense that assemblies start in the classroom as the children get ready to leave their classrooms.
- That they come to assembly quietly and enter knowing how and where they should sit down.
- That the leader of assembly is waiting for the children and if possible is seated, being able to have eye contact with the children as they sit down.
- An appropriate themed display and calming music playing in order to create a 'conscious assembly' where adults and children can be fully present.
- That all staff model the behaviour that they are expecting from the children by sitting quietly with a focus on the leader of the assembly.

I don't wish to imply that there can't be lively, entertaining sections of the assembly, but I think it's important at the end to ensure that everyone can calm themselves and leave in the way that they entered.

A former head of Ledbury Primary School, Julie Rees, had a wonderful chair, I called it her throne, which she sat on at the beginning and end of assemblies – inspirational!

Of course, you must adapt assemblies to your school's context and your own style of teaching, but the important point is that in conducting an assembly you are acting as a role model, not only for the value you are talking about but all the school's values. Staff and students will spot any inconsistencies between what you say and you do.

I also witnessed the above point, about modelling the values vocabulary, when I visited Hill Farm Primary School in Coventry, because the school had applied for the Values Enhanced Quality Mark. This outstanding VbE school has given a great deal of thought about developing the curriculum holistically, with key elements connected to each other. The school has an inspirational way of embedding values under five themes that are expressed with the mnemonic LEARN: Live without harm, Equal opportunities, Altruism, Resourcefulness, Navigate the world. The five British values (democracy, rule of law, individual liberty, mutual respect, tolerance of those with different faiths and beliefs) that are legally required in English schools are found within this model, as are the school's chosen twenty values. This is the first school that I have visited where altruism is talked about in Early Years. In the photo, I am presenting the school with the Enhanced Values Quality Mark.

I observed an outstanding Socratic-style lesson on trust, where the students talked about when they felt they could trust someone. The teacher implicitly used the values vocabulary when interacting with her students. She used remarks such as, "Yes, empathy is so important in relationships." She ended the

FIGURE 10.1 The Enhanced Values Quality Mark

lesson saying, "Thank you all for showing such respect to each other's opinions during the lesson." She skilfully held the space for the students – an authentic model of a conscious classroom.

Children agreed that it takes a long time to build up real trust in another person, but they argued that you must initially give some trust in a relationship but that real lasting trust develops over time. The students showed ethical, emotional and critical intelligence in the mature way they addressed the value of trust, showing that they had been given numerous opportunities to reflect and think deeply about life issues.

One highlight of many on this school visit was when the values ambassadors met with me to explain their role and talk about the importance of values at the school. They had an exceptional knowledge about the nature of values and were fully conscious about how they help their thinking and behaviour both at school and at home. They felt confident to share some of their own personal stories, which showed how they felt safe and secure in their relationships with staff. One ambassador said, "It's a very big role, and we are trusted to give awards to pupils who are role models, showing their values." When asked how they use their values in lessons, another said, "It's important to use values such as determination, so that we can do our best and learn well." At home, they said they used their values to help their parents, such as in keeping their bedroom tidy. What was so impressive was that the values were talked about so naturally.

At the end of the day, parents were invited to hear from the children about what they had been learning in school. Students confidently articulated their thoughts about values and other aspects of the curriculum. Values certificates were given to students who that week had shown a particular value. One boy showed me his certificate and glowed with pride as he told me that he had been given one for being brave with his learning and making a massive improvement with his handwriting.

Time for your thoughts

- When do you create time for children to think about the role values play in our lives?
- If you are a school leader or teacher, how do you ensure that your class or school assemblies are inspiring, enjoyable and a community enhancing experience?
- How and when could you use the values vocabulary implicitly when talking with children?

11

A focus on mental wellbeing and health, emphasising care and compassion

The global decline in mental wellbeing and health is acknowledged as a huge problem. Increasingly children are being diagnosed with a range of health issues that put a strain on resources to provide appropriate provision in mainstream schools. In this chapter you will be able to reflect on how some schools are creating the best possible environment that is mindful about the mental wellbeing and health of all students and staff. The conscious classroom creates the ethos, relationships and routines that support the mental wellbeing and health of students and staff. At Worplesdon Primary School, they think carefully about the support they give to children who present as having concerns, as is exemplified in these case studies.

DOI: 10.4324/9781003681144-11

Child A

Concern: Fear of failure when speaking in a performance, very self-conscious.

Action: Embedded in the child's thinking, the use of focal point when speaking in a performance. To build resilience, we gradually built this up over time until child became confident speaking in front of adults. Child A wanted to join a club and learn a new language. Again, we broke this down to a ladder of success each week for the child to work independently on the task. First the child completed the new language, then with the use of exchanging red words for green (negative/positive words) and positive affirmations, in time the child started to feel a sense of belonging. Affirmation work was daily and progress was fed back to the teacher weekly. Over time, child A said, "I believe in myself and I am enough." When Child A left the school, a revisit took place after three months and the following was shared, "I came back as I wanted to share with you that I have joined a club and took part in a performance already. I knew you would be proud of my determination, resilience and positivity."

Child B

Concern: Child lacked role models and sense of self.

Action: We looked at all values and have been working on a value per month. Child came up with ideas of how they could show that value. The child independently went home and acknowledged values with family; child now praises family when they are themselves sharing values in the community.

Child C

Concern: Child lacked confidence in ability, angry reaction to failure.

Action: We looked at what the child would like to achieve and the steps to get to that point. The child independently worked weekly on each stage of a process to get to the top of a ladder to success. At each point, we celebrated the value around the success. When at the top of the ladder, the child said, "I did it, I want to show everyone, I can do it and I am really proud."

These case studies exemplify how conscious classrooms are aware of the individual needs of students, deeply listening to them and responding appropriately with helpful support, such as where the presence of an animal helps a child to feel happy and calm.

The key is to create an ethos in which students feel that they have a good relationship with adults and can share their concerns. From my own experience as a teacher and from my observations of others, I have been convinced that open, honest, caring communication with children is the foundation for authentic, meaningful relationships. These in turn are the foundation for positively influencing and inspiring young people to experiment with their understanding about what values such as courage, confidence and determination mean in their lives. With such insights, they can then work towards an understanding about who they want to be in the world, which is the foundation of values-based conscious classrooms, conscious self-leadership and a flourishing world.

Staff wellbeing is also a key element of conscious values-led schools. This is exemplified at Hinkley Parks Primary School in Leicestershire. Staff wellbeing is actively promoted and led by a member of the senior leadership team (SLT). Initiatives include whole days for team planning, time off to get COVID vaccinations and organisation of a weekly food van in recognition for their hard work and dedication. All staff support the values ethos of the academy, and staff feel highly valued. Wellbeing of staff and students is very evident in the school, and individuals are supported so that they feel a valued part of the school community. An example was the excellent circus that was arranged for students and staff to experience and enjoy. Giving children opportunities to develop holistically by giving them access to such creative experiences is much appreciated by parents, who told me that what the school does to enrich the curriculum is appreciated by them.

The headteacher wrote in his values enhanced audit report that:

> Staff wellbeing has been a key focus, especially during the challenging time we had during lockdown. Staff workload was considered while planning home learning and pre-recorded lessons were used to remove pressure. Staff-parents who were working from home also commented that it helped them as they didn't have to stick to a time when a live lesson was on and could fit in home learning around their commitments.
>
> Since returning to in-school learning, staff were surveyed on the different methods we had in place to support wellbeing, and changes were made to further support staff.

> INSET training was organised and delivered at the start of this year. 'Journey to Better Mental Health' to allow staff to learn or revisit strategies to support them.
>
> All our staff have access to wellbeing support, including: an open door policy to discuss issues with senior management; the option to have school dinners; free tea and coffee in the staff room; a dedicated work area for PPA; talk therapy and fast tracker referrals for physiotherapy.

These are a few examples, but the main point I would wish to emphasise is that conscious schools really do think carefully about wellbeing and avoid tokenism. There is a danger in schools which are continually striving to do more rather than *be* more. They can add to mental ill-health, which is increasing in society because of multiple, complex, inter-related reasons: including concerns about the economy, use of social media, world news, climate change, increase in a variety of conditions associated with special educational needs, changes in parenting and childhood experiences, etc.

The school cannot directly ease all the pressures on carers, parents, communities and society at large, but it can show how conscious classrooms can create an ethos that is calm, positive, happy and purposeful, where there is time to listen deeply to how children are experiencing their lives and to give regular times to P2B. Such awareness of the needs of children as human beings ensures that communication skills are fostered in an atmosphere of harmonious relationships, enabling students to express themselves clearly and with confidence. Conscious classrooms enable students to develop what I describe as an enhanced consciousness based on human intelligences, such as ethical intelligence, which are profoundly needed to navigate successfully in a supercomplex world whilst holding on to their mental integrity.

Thinking about wellbeing

- How are you taking care of you?

Note down all that you do and would like to do. Act on your to-do list. Remember you help others best if you help yourself first. This is what can be called ‘wise selfishness’.

- What could you do to improve children’s wellbeing?

12

A quality learning environment and empowering curriculum that gives a sense of safety and dignity

As discussed in the previous chapter, a key feature of conscious schools that reduce stress and anxiety is that they consciously create a learning environment where all feel that their dignity is intact, and they feel safe and secure. In this chapter, we will consider what these schools do.

As best as it can, a conscious classroom creates a quality, humane learning environment. By this I mean that thought has been given, for instance, to the arrangement of furniture and resources based on how the children best learn – age- and stage-appropriate. For me, the outdoors is an integral part of the learning environment, where there are ample opportunities for younger children to explore and be engaged in purposeful and imaginative play.

DOI: 10.4324/9781003681144-12

A conscious classroom challenges ideas that may be rooted in a bygone age. Research shows that children learn most effectively if they have first-hand experiences, such as visits to local landmarks – museums, religious buildings, farms, etc. Writing with a purpose to the local council or businesses makes writing real, as does writing creatively to produce a real book. The same can be said about creative work in the arts, where communication is enhanced through drama and imagination and nurtured through drawing and painting. Science, mathematics and critical thinking are used when children explore big ideas that have created our civilisation. Such a hands-on pedagogy leaves the child feeling proud of what they achieve whilst learning many skills and developing enhancing character traits. Such conscious classrooms give children a sense of safety and dignity, which is the value of having inherent self-worth.

Roecroft Lower School in Bedfordshire is an excellent example of a school that thinks deeply about creating a quality learning environment. The photo shows that any visitor is

FIGURE 12.1 Roecroft Lower School is proud to be a values-based school. The writing on the door proclaims that it fosters quality learning.

made aware that they are entering a values-based school by the message on the front door.

Inside, displays and samples of children's work show that learning through Values-based Education is planned around key questions or concepts that deepen and broaden student knowledge and understanding, with examples coming from the regular values mornings and values displays.

The school is a very safe place to be, which helps children to feel relaxed but alert to do their best during lessons. The quality of displays around Roecroft is inspiring, creating an ambiance that encourages students to be the best people that they can be. The school is well ordered; there is amazing

FIGURE 12.2 Smiling eyes at Roecroft school underpin excellent staff pupil relationships.

attention to detail, and every space is used to good effect. I was delighted to have lunch with the chair of governors, who explained how committed the governing body is to being the critical friend that enables positive development in the school.

I have found it hard to select examples from so many schools that are making a profound difference in children's lives, as the family of values-based conscious schools is now so diverse and wide-ranging geographically. Please forgive me if your school is not mentioned in this book by me – you are still highly valued!

However, having admitted my unease with selecting examples, I would like you to hear about Bannockburn Primary School in the Plumstead area of London, which is a great example of a school that I am proud to call a conscious school. It has been awarded the Enhanced Values Quality Mark. It is an example of an urban school in a multicultural area that has responded positively to creating a quality, inclusive, learning environment, with a relevant curriculum that responds to its community.

I thought you would be interested to read what the school wrote in its self-audit.

Bannockburn primary school's vision: "Growing together, learning for life."

We do this through:

- Promoting mutual respect and positive values.
- Facing new challenges together through teamwork.
- Learning and achieving in a supportive, stimulating, and creative environment.

- Celebrating diversity and working in partnership with parents and the wider community.

At Bannockburn Primary School we want every child to be successful; to reach for success from the very first day they join us and throughout their school lives, so that when they leave us, they have a love of learning for the rest of their lives. Our moral compass is intertwined through our curriculum through our internal moral compass.

Bannockburn Primary School strives to:

- Deliver a well-balanced, creative curriculum tailored to the needs of every child based on the National Curriculum and the Foundation Stage Curriculum.
- Be friendly, happy and hardworking.
- Deliver outstandingly high-quality teaching and learning.
- Encourage and nurture positive attitudes towards work.
- Develop respect and understanding for others.
- Provide a stimulating, caring, supportive and safe environment.
- Encourage our children to become confident, independent learners who respond positively to challenge.
- Encourage our children to have the confidence to explore and experiment as they work to develop their skills and talents.
- Facilitate a range of sporting, musical and extra-curricular activities which enrich our curriculum.
- Celebrate the achievements of all children, both in and out of school.
- Encourage each individual to take responsibility for their own behaviour and to act as good role models to others.

Bannockburn Primary School has balloted parent/carers, governors and children to extend the original 11 values to 22.

FIGURE 12.3 Values wrist bands given to students who display the school's values.

Every value has a designated, coloured wristband, worn by the adults to remind everyone of the value of the month.

Quotations from meeting with parents include:

> The school listens to the children and their opinions. Pupil voice is listened to and acted upon.
>
> I am comfortable that my daughters are respected by other children (wearing a turban); there is consistency across both sites and adults deal with any inappropriate comments.
>
> All religions are acknowledged by the school. When my daughter suggested last year's Assembly on Sikhism and Diwali would be better as two separate ones, the school changed them so that this year they were.

International Evening is great! Cultures, food and talents are shared.

My child is at a very inclusive school.

In my report about the school for the Values Quality Mark, I wrote:

> Ethos is about the quality of the culture of a school and its individuals. The unique culture of a school is composed of the character of the staff and the values that they model.
>
> Bannockburn Primary School has an outstanding values-based ethos as the school's self-evaluation highlights. The Headteacher, Senior Leadership Team and all staff model the values of the school. This creates a trusting and harmonious environment where pupils feel safe and happy.
>
> The staff are highly supportive of each other, and staff wellbeing is a strength of the school. The innovative wellbeing sessions for staff are highly valued. One member of staff, who had worked in several schools, said that he had never experienced such a friendly and supportive school.
>
> The ethos is calm, happy and purposeful. Adults speak to pupils respectfully and kindly. Pupil behaviour is exemplary.

FIGURE 12.4 The energy, enthusiasm and dedication of staff, exampled by the music teacher, creates a school values culture where students thrive.

> SEND pupils are skilfully supported. Pupils are treated as individuals and welcomed for who they are as people.
>
> The school's values are at the heart of the school's ethos, and the school community has trust in the school.
>
> Teaching staff are enthusiastic and great role models as this teacher exemplified during a singing Assembly.

In the recent report for Bannockburn Primary School (June 2025), Ofsted wrote:

> Pupils understand the importance of the school's values. They actively look for opportunities to demonstrate them, such as being a good role model, and displaying kindness and positivity to others.

Congratulations to all in Bannockburn's community and, indeed, all schools that are creating quality learning environments and empowering a curriculum that gives a sense of safety and dignity, and of course quality learning experiences.

Thinking about the classroom environment

Have a few moments of blue-sky thinking . . .

- What's your ideal teaching environment. What does it look like?

Now think about your current teaching environment . . .

- What changes will you make to move it towards your ideal?

13

Excellent staff relationships with each other, students and the community

As a leader, a priority of mine has been to create the conditions where harmonious relationships can thrive. This chapter will invite you to consider the ways some schools foster good relationships.

Former British Prime Minister Tony Blair once prioritised education by boldly saying, "Education, education and education," viewing it as a key to economic success. Though when giving presentations on VbE, I have always given another perspective by saying that, "Education is about relationships, relationships and relationships."

If I were to reduce this book to a single sentence, I would write that conscious classrooms are outstanding learning environments because of the quality of relationships established between staff and students. I have had the privilege of visiting thousands of schools during my career, and I have yet to visit a school of quality that hasn't got good relationships at its core.

DOI: 10.4324/9781003681144-13

If we have positive, meaningful connections with other people, we learn and thrive because we feel safe and connected. This is because there is a natural flow of embodied energy between adults and children.

A key feature of a conscious school is making good relationships central to its ethos. They are not easy to maintain, demanding that we use as much emotional intelligence as we can muster. As complex beings, we are often challenged to maintain good relationships both with ourselves and others. To support schools when they are worried about relationships, I often recommend Don Miguel Ruiz's book *The Four Agreements* (Amber-Allen, 1997). Without going into detail, the book outlines four agreements that I keep with myself and find so affirming. If I may share them with you: "Be impeccable with your word," "Don't take anything personally," "Don't make assumptions" and last "Always do your best."

As a staff, giving time to talking about how to maintain good relationships with each other gives opportunity for open, respectful, honest discussion and informal and perhaps formal procedures which will help to heal relationships if they begin to break down. Values such as dignity are central to such discussions, as such a value highlights and reminds us of the inherent self-worth of each member of staff. I advise that there should never be a hierarchy of relationships in a school, only of roles, so everyone feels that they are equal as human beings and that their voices are valued.

Values-based schools emphasise good relationships, as I will illustrate in the following example, which typifies schools that are evolving their consciousness.

Under its previous headteacher, Charlotte Hickerton, St Peter at Gowts CE Primary School in Lincoln is a faith-based school that adopted VbE to underpin the school's curriculum and pedagogy. Relationships were central to the leadership's strategy for success in this outward-facing school. Pedagogy is about how children are taught and how they access learning. This school achieves something that I've rarely seen in my experience. The school had constructed a curriculum that went well beyond meeting statutory requirements. The basic curriculum is well taught; the school adds value by ensuring that it is planned to engage with the interests of the children and the big real issues that they face in their lives, preparing them for their future lives. Values in action and really lived! In Year 5, I saw an excellent example of the quality of the school's relational pedagogy, encouraging children to think deeply about matters of significance.

The students were using the learning strategies and methods embodied in Philosophy for Children (P4C) and conflict

FIGURE 13.1 School values being lived by students in the community.

resolution. The lesson was helping the children to develop their ethical intelligence: the ability to ethically self-regulate their behaviour. The children showed the self-discipline to get the most out of their learning and enjoy harmonious relationships.

The ethos in the room was highly respectful of the opinions of others, and the children showed that they were able to build on the ideas of others. They were encouraged to be reflective, to consider their thinking and construct an argument – all higher-order thinking skills displaying the students' critical intelligence. They thought about wisdom and how two children in Year 6 had been wise when they reported to adults that they had seen a knife under a car. The boys had been commended by the police and were featured in the local press. The question that the students then skilfully debated was whether you could teach someone to be wise.

I witnessed such higher-order thinking skills in all classes and in individual and group work, such as Year 6 thinking about ethical dilemmas. The teacher asked the students to gather round in groups, each group being given an ethical dilemma to consider and told that there were no right or wrong answers but situations where we need to dig deep and respond from our values – our bottom line!

No one felt shamed when offering their thinking, and each other's dignity was maintained. The group, discussing the dilemma in the photo on the next page, unanimously said that they wouldn't cheat. I have used this dilemma with groups of adults and been amazed how many have said that they would cheat, whereas when I challenged the Year 6 children, they said that they would not cheat because they had learned about the importance of living their values, which their teachers had been teaching them about. A warm, friendly, calm atmosphere with children focused on their learning permeated this amazing conscious school.

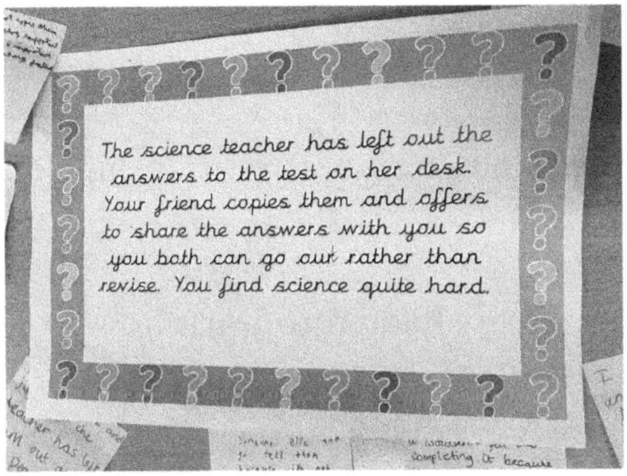

FIGURE 13.2 Ethical dilemma: would you cheat?

St Peter's at Gowts is a school that is constantly reaching out to its community through links such as the family support staff. The school spares no effort to engage with families to work in an active partnership for the benefit of the children but also of the families and the community. The governors and diocese give every encouragement to the school being a beacon of values-based education.

My hope is that others will be inspired by this and other case study schools, understanding how a conscious school, with its conscious classrooms raises real standards, in terms of behaving as an altruistic human being, knowing who you want to be in the world and who cares deeply for the well-being of others.

This school also features an impressive values sculpture of two trees that welcomes students at the school gates, symbolising the school's outward-facing and inclusive nature.

I wrote at the conclusion of my audit report of the school:

> This is a school that is a microcosm of what the world could be.

Pause and reflect?

Building and maintaining good relationships takes deliberate effort.

- How do you help children to learn how to get along with others (age- and stage-appropriate)?
- What information could you use or adapt from this chapter in your setting?

14

Excellent behaviour and agency of students who live their values

The previous chapter's focus on relationships neatly prepares the ground for considering how conscious classrooms foster good behaviour and agency, not only in formal settings.

Coming to this chapter, I realise that all the previous examples of conscious classrooms are excellent illustrations of schools that have excellent student behaviour, where children have agency, taking responsibility for their learning and behaviour, and do their best to live the values that the school is teaching them about.

However, students may find themselves out of mainstream schooling for a variety of reasons and their experience of a conscious classroom is not in a traditional setting.

Some have been permanently excluded because of their challenging behaviour and risk being marginalised by society. Therefore, I think it's appropriate to focus in this chapter on an excellent example of alternative provision.

DOI: 10.4324/9781003681144-14

I was contacted by Support'ed, based in Plymouth, that offers support alongside secondary school-aged students, tailor-making a curriculum for them with one-to-one support. Values are at the heart of the organisation's methods, and it applied for the Values Quality Mark. Support'ed has a calm, purposeful and friendly atmosphere. A great sense of teamwork and commitment pervades the organisation. Leadership is highly reflected and values led – a good example of conscious leadership.

Great care is taken to ensure that each young person is treated fairly and honestly in an open person-centred environment. Jane and I acted as assessors and spent a day observing the richness of provision, ranging from cookery to visits to the beach to look at marine life, Thai boxing sessions and accompanying members of staff on home visits.

Support'ed has selected what's referred to as the eight Cs as the core of its ethical vocabulary. These are: clarity, compassion, courage, confidence, curiosity, creativity, calmness and connection. These particular values are sometimes referred to as the qualities of our authentic self, the qualities we show when we are being authentically ourselves.

The way that this ethical vocabulary is being used is by helping 'challenged' young people to develop their ethical intelligence: the ability to ethically self-regulate their behaviour.

It also supports the development of personal holistic competence (PHC), which is a term I use to describe the ability to address complexity in our lives with confidence by drawing on a range of skills, capacities and qualities of character. These two elements may seem to you remote and academic, but when seen in action, as we did in the Thai boxing session, they really do come alive.

For instance, when an older student spoke to us after his Thai boxing bout, he shared with us that, because of the values that Support'ed espouse, he was taking control of himself, able to reflect on his behaviour. It was very moving when he described what he wanted his future to look like. He was setting himself a meaning and purpose for his life, which he could only do because he is finding himself through his positive relationship with his teacher, who is inspiring him to be the best version of himself that he can be. Because he is big, he said that he was picked on in mainstream schooling to prove that he was strong. Fights led to his exclusion. He said that it was only when he came to Support'ed that he was really listened to and felt seen. Now, he was gaining in confidence, walking away from trouble and helping others as a Thai boxing student coach. In the photo, he is teaching Jane.

On a home visit, a parent of another student shared with me that Support'ed was the first organisation that had come

FIGURE 14.1 A student teaching Jane

alongside her son with positive values, which was allowing him to take his first real steps to being able to flourish as a person. Sadly, in her view, she catalogued how the social and education systems had failed her son, who has specific behavioural and learning needs. Conversely, Support'ed had come alongside him and her family, giving them hope for his future.

Being with the dynamic team at Support'ed was inspirational and showed what can be done for young people whom the system rejects and society marginalises. Consciously putting the young person's needs at the centre of the curriculum and support is key to unlocking their hidden potential. As we were told, "It is at Support'ed where I have found respect and have been listen to."

The Support'ed director, Tim George, gave a great insight into the balance that staff face in maintaining relationships with students:

> At Support'ed, we recognise that working in a truly values–led way involves a constant balance between keeping young people safe, and allowing them space to develop independence and voice. Sharing control can feel uncomfortable, particularly when responsibility, risk and safeguarding are at the forefront of our work. For many staff, the instinct to take control comes not from a desire for power (there have been some for whom this is the case), but from care, uncertainty and a fear of getting things wrong. When confidence is still developing, control can feel the safest option.

I'm sure Tim's remarks will ring true with so many readers who wish to give agency to students.

At the end of the audit day, Jane and I had no hesitation in awarding the Values-based Quality Mark to this outstanding and inspirational organisation. In this instance, the conscious classroom exists in the respectful, caring and authentic relationships between students and staff.

Questions for you to consider

- In your experience what are the keys to foster good behaviour?
- What can you do to increase agency in young people?

15

Values-based Education being lived and celebrated in the school and community

Wow! You have reached my tenth and final insight, which is about living and celebrating VbE as your way of creating conscious classrooms.

Some years ago, I audited Whalley Range 11–18 High School in Manchester for the Values Quality Mark. I still vividly remember the visit, because the students were relaxed, happy, focused and alert and therefore gained from the excellent standard of teaching. Members of the school's council displayed an outstanding level of communicative competence, being able to articulate the importance of values in school and in their lives. They really did celebrate and live the tenets of VbE, as they displayed in their self-awareness when discussing in a group. Without exception, they lived the school's values and had excellent manners and interpersonal skills.

DOI: 10.4324/9781003681144-15

This aspect of consciousness is rooted in primary VbE schools, where simple skills such as 'batting it back' can be taught. This helps children to understand that if someone greets you, you greet them back. "How are you today?" "I'm very well, thank you. How are you?"

The headteacher of a Coventry primary school shared with me that making her students conscious about such social enhancement techniques had helped her students to be more concerned about others and less self-absorbed.

The power of making values fully conscious in classrooms, which then filters into homes and the community, was highlighted to me when talking with a parent at Trumacar Nursery and Primary School in Lancashire. I would like to share with you what she said:

> I think respect and value is learnt behaviour. Children learn what they see. So, I think the fact that such a high value is put on respect, tolerance, awareness and quality of people must filter home. But I think that some homes do not have the respect and values, because perhaps they didn't have that stability in life. I think that for some homes, the values the children learn here is fed through to the parents and, sometimes, as a parent myself, I've had to stop and think, "Yes, what they are actually saying is right" and I think it is very good, as a parent, to be kept on your toes. Because the children are given such value as their Trumacar Family, they identified how to bring that into the home and that's a gift you can't buy.

School assemblies, especially when they involve parents, give schools opportunities to celebrate the living of values. At Chantry Primary Academy in Luton, I recently witnessed such an assembly. A special moment for me was when students received their values certificates for displaying their values. An older student dressed up as a magic fairy and, with her wand, sprinkled stardust on the recipients.

At the same school, the children take their values into the community. Cori Bateman, the CEO of the Pioneer Trust, of which the school is a part, says,

> "Chantry's children are not just values-based, they are brave and outspoken advocates for a values-based world, where everyone feels the impact of values-based behaviours."

For me, this is the key outcome of the conscious classroom: that values are not just talked about but are embedded in the students' consciousness so that they naturally act as courageous advocates, promoting a humane, equitable and peaceful world where all can flourish.

Your insights

I have laid my dreams, experience and insights at your feet for your consideration. The fact that you have read my book to this point gives me the confidence to assume that you are finding it helpful to you in whatever role you play.

Before moving on to the final chapter, may I invite you to consider, in addition to my thoughts, how you would raise consciousness in students. I would love to hear your ideas, which could help us to put conscious classrooms at the centre of educational debate and practice.

16

A heartfelt message to the future

Wow! We've reached the final chapter on our journey into discovering the transformational properties of the conscious classroom, and why they should be established in all schools, colleges, universities and other educational settings.

However, before you continue reading, may I invite you to revisit 'Welcome from Neil', the introduction to the book. I suggest this because I understand that some readers may miss out introductions, proceeding to begin their engagement with a book at Chapter 1.

In my Welcome, I outlined the rationale for the book and why I have been motivated to write it. To herald a new form of leadership and governance in the world, I emphasised that we need to educate our young people to acquire the dispositions of character that will nurture their ethical intelligence, which is their ability to ethically self-regulate their thinking and behaviour. This form of education will enhance the natural essence of us, which is based on human values such as empathy, compassion, love, peace, truth, dignity, care and justice.

DOI: 10.4324/9781003681144-16

I hope you have felt my passion and commitment to this form of education, which is based on my lifetime as an educator. I put this passion, embodied energy, into my TEDx talk on Values-based Education. I feel humbled that so many people have watched it globally and, I'm told, have used it to inspire others. I remember the day of the talk in 2018 so clearly. As a presenter, I'm not used to having to prepare a script, which the organisation recommended to deliver the talk in the prescribed time. Alarmingly, in practising the talk in front of my wife Jane, she told me I would be a disaster, because I wasn't being the usual authentic, enthusiastic, inspiring me but a second-rate script reader.

I tore up the speech and decided to note the headings of what I wanted to say but that on the day I would speak from my heart. On reflection, I can tell you that the talk turned out to be probably the most demanding I have ever given. For in front of me on the stage was a clock that counted down the 16 minutes of my allotted time. At 3 minutes to go, it turned red and started flashing! Would I get to the conclusion of my talk in time?

I did but, uncharacteristically, when I sat down with Jane, I felt emotionally overwhelmed, tears rolling down my cheeks and my hands shaking. You see I had invested the whole of me into the talk, because I could see its vital importance as a way of reaching out to a wide audience. If you watch my TEDx talk, I wonder if you will spot my heightened energy towards its conclusion.

In the dynamic photo of me on the next page, I am in a similar position to Francesca, the student who's under the globe in the picture. I was explaining to the audience that the arms of the values globe sculpture, which is outside West Kidlington School, show the hands of children from the five continents, who are holding up

FIGURE 16.1 "Our children's values will hold up our world." Neil's inspirational TEDx talk which has attracted thousands of views globally.

our world with their values. If future generations do not have enabling values, then our world will not be held up, will collapse and fail to flourish.

Coincidentally, whilst writing this chapter, I was contacted by a former student who was one of the children who made the sculpture. His email moved me and emphasised how, as teachers, our energy can have a profound effect on our students. Bruce has given me permission to share an extract with you:

Dear Dr Hawkes,

My name is Bruce Wilson and I am a former pupil at West Kidlington Primary School. I attended the school between 1994 and 2000, following in the footsteps of my brother, Tom, who was a few years older than me. I remember your values-based assemblies very fondly, and – although not explicitly aware of this as a child – believe that they helped me find my 'true north'. I remember the values of the month, the construction of the 'world in our hands', the quiet reflection times – sometimes with a candle, the whole-school singing and the community this created. My children, currently 3 and 5, now attend the school and are in Nursery and Year 1, and I simply love rekindling memories about my time there. They stand very proudly next to the 'world in our hands' at the front of school and say, "My daddy helped build this!". . .

Very recently, I was made aware that what was happening at West Kidlington, at the time of your headship and my childhood, was not 'ordinary' but actually something very special, profound and way ahead of its time . . .

I would be honoured if I could book you, as I take up my Headship, for a September INSET day to share your vision for values-based education. I can't think of a more 'full-circle' moment than to have my old Headteacher helping me get off to the best possible start as a Head myself.

From the bottom of my heart, thank you.

Kind regards
Bruce

Hearing that a former pupil will now continue my mission in his first headship is testimony to the power of VbE if it is used as the basis for creating conscious classrooms.

The reason I'm sharing these personal stories with you is that I want to emphasise the crucial role that our unseen energy plays in our lives. In my TEDx presentation, I had failed to be sufficiently Self-aware to manage my own energy successfully!

When we are alive, we radiate energy – we are embodied energy. It's literally our energy that makes things happen for us in our lives – for good or ill. Mastering it reaps great rewards in terms of our experience of life and how we are driven to live out our existence. Others sense our energy. For instance, on entering a room, it's possible to feel the energy which individuals or the group is creating. I expect you will have experienced that feeling of being able to cut the atmosphere with a knife.

If we are Self-aware, as this book explains how to be in Chapter 4, then we realise when we are projecting energy that may be harmful to others and quickly become the objective observer of ourselves to manage our energy. We are then more aware, conscious of those aspects of our personality which may be sabotaging us and our relationships. In such circumstances, we breathe deeply, allowing our internal system to settle. Then we focus on the root of our energy, our essence, our wise Self, which will guide us in our thinking and behaviour. It's our innate wisdom that we all have but is sadly so often marginalised by those ego-driven aspects of our personality.

I hope you find this explanation about energy helpful, as an understanding of it will support you, your own Self-energy, as you consider the process that students go through in a conscious classroom.

If we can channel our energy to raise our consciousness level of awareness based on living human values that empower us, then I can see real hope for humans to flourish in the future. I am in awe of the leaders and teachers in so many schools whom I witness transforming their schools into a new paradigm – bringing the future into the present. This is despite external systems that constrain them. I have highlighted many of these leaders and teachers in this book, but there are thousands more, and others who are on the tipping point of joining the *Quiet Revolution* of the heart.

My vision for the future is that educational environments, which are not all called schools, focus on accepting the dignity, the inherent self-worth of all students and the adults who work with them; that there is a deep understanding about how we can nurture those aspects of us that lead to self-actualisation and altruistic agency; that students are helped to have an understanding about who they are and who they choose to be in the world, as I outlined in Chapter 1.

My hope is that students will realise the incredible gifts that education, through conscious classrooms, bestows on them, having been given the opportunity to develop their potential, by realising their talents and their abilities across the curriculum. My hope is that they have a teacher, as I did in Mr Blacksell at secondary school, who told shy me that he wanted me to play Hotspur in the school's Shakespeare production of *Henry IV, Part 1.* His belief in me, his enthusiasm and his skilled tutoring transformed me and my life, because from that time on I found that inner belief, that spark of creative energy, which gave meaning, purpose and guidance throughout my life.

Teachers are so often heroes because they send messages to the future, in the sense that their teaching helps form young people into adults. I recall a professor of education at Tartu University in Estonia chatting with me on one of my visits to the country about how we can assess the success of education. In our conversation, she paused briefly and then said that the only real assessment is to ask ten or twenty years later, "What are the people like in our society? Are they contributing to a healthy, compassionate, vibrant society or are they self-interested, and blind to the needs of others and our planet."

Are the world's current systems of educating students leading to a realisation of my vision? I'll leave the answer for you to decide.

If you agree with me that conscious classrooms should be the norm in our schools, then how will you help to bring this about?

A favour, when you have finished with this book: please don't leave it on a shelf; share it with someone else who may also use the ideas. Alternatively, give it away and buy another! We can achieve our ambition for conscious schools if we multiply our influence.

A huge thank you for being with me on this book's journey. I hope you have enjoyed reading it as much as I have been inspired through writing it.

In gratitude,
Neil

Bibliography

Benedict, Anthony and Braven, Alan. (2025). *Educating Everyone: An Introduction to Relational Inclusion.* London: Taylor & Francis.

Costa, Arthur L. and Killick, Bena. (2008). *Learning and Leading with Habits of Mind.* Alexandria, VA: ASCD.

Farrer, Frances. (2000). *A Quiet Revolution: Encouraging Positive Values in Our Children.* London: Random.

Hawkes, Neil. (1977). *Home, School and Community Relationships with Special Reference to a Village Primary School.* M.Ed. Thesis (unpublished). Reading University.

Hawkes, Neil. (2003). *How to Inspire and Develop Values in Your Classroom.* Cambridge: LDA.

Hawkes, Neil. (2005) *Does Teaching about Values Improve the Quality of Education in Primary Schools?* Doctoral Thesis. Department of Education, Oxford University.

Hawkes, Neil. (2010). *Does Teaching Values Improve the Quality of Education in Primary Schools? A Study about the Impact of Introducing Values Education in a Primary School.* Beau-Bassin, Mauritius: VDM Publishing House.

Hawkes, Neil. (2013). *From My Heart: Transforming Lives through Values.* Carmarthen, Independent Thinking Press.

Hawkes, Neil and Jane, Hawkes. (2018). *The Inner Curriculum: How to Nourish Wellbeing, Resilience and Self-Leadership.* Melton: John Catt Educational.

Lovat, Terence J., Toomey, Ron, Clement, Neville and Dally, Kerry. (2023). *Second international Research Handbook on Values Education and Student Wellbeing.* Melbourne, Vic: Springer Nature.

Lovat, Terence J., Toomey, Ron, Dally, Kerry and Clement, Neville. (2009). *Project to Test and Measure the Impact of Values Education on Student Effects and School Ambience.* Report for the Australian Government Department of Education, Employment and Workplace Relations (DEEWR) by the University of Newcastle, Australia.

Newman, Andrew S. (2016 onwards). *Conscious Stories* series. Nashville, TN: Conscious Stories LLC.

Ofsted. (1997). West Kidlington Primary School, Inspection Report. School Register Number: 123004. Reporting Inspector: Ms J Morris. Inspection carried out under Section 10 of the Education (Schools) Act 1996.

Palmer, Parker J. (1997). *The Courage to Teach: Exploring the Inner Landscape of a Teacher's Life.* San Francisco, CA: Jossey-Bass.

Reay, Andrew. (2017). *The Power of Character: Lessons from the Frontline.* Melton: John Catt Educational Ltd.

Ricard, Mathieu. (2015). *Altruism.* London: Atlantic Books.

Ruiz, Don Miguel. (1997). *The Four Agreements.* San Rafael, CA: Amber-Allen.

Schwartz, Richard C. (1995). *Internal Family Systems Therapy.* New York: Guilford Press.

Schwartz, Richard C. (2001). *Introduction to the Internal Family Systems Model.* Illinois: Trailheads, Division of The Centre for Self Leadership.

Siegel Daniel J. (1999). *The Developing Mind: How Relationships and the Brain Interact to Shape Who We Are: Towards a Neurobiology of Interpersonal Experience.* New York: Guilford Press.

Siegel, Daniel J. (2007). *The Mindful Brain.* New York: WW Norton.

Tillman, Diane G. (1996). *Living Values: An Educational Program.* Deerfield, FL: Health Communications Inc.

Viegas, Marneta. (2000 onwards). *Relax Kids* series. London: Collective Ink.

Williams Mark A. (2023). *The Connected Species.* Lanham, MD: Rowman & Littlefield.

Woodrow, Floyd. (2016). *The Warrior, the Strategist and You.* London: Elliott & Thompson.

Woodrow, Floyd. (2017). *Compass for Life.* London: Elliott & Thompson.

Index

INDEX

INDEX

INDEX

INDEX

INDEX

INDEX

INDEX

INDEX

INDEX

For Product Safety Concerns and Information please contact our EU representative GPSR@taylorandfrancis.com
Taylor & Francis Verlag GmbH, Kaufingerstraße 24, 80331 München, Germany

www.ingramcontent.com/pod-product-compliance
Lightning Source LLC
LaVergne TN
LVHW021322070826
845179LV00023B/306

9781041157687